Published by MJF Books
Fine Communications
322 Eighth Avenue
New York, NY 10001

Money Matters
LC Control Number 2006933335
ISBN-13: 978-1-56731-835-7
ISBN-10: 1-56731-835-5

Copyright © 2004 by Dave Ramsey

Originally published by J. Countryman, a Division of Thomas Nelson, Inc., under the title *The Money Answer Book*. This edition published by MJF Books in arrangement with J. Countryman, a Division of Thomas Nelson, Inc.

New Century Version of the Bible (NCV) copyright © 1987, 1988, 1991 by Thomas Nelson, Inc. All rights reserved.

The New International Version of the Bible (NIV) copyright © 1984 by the International Bible Society. Used by permission of Zondervan Bible Publishers.

Project Editor: Kathy Baker
Designed by Brand Navigation, Sisters, Oregon

All rights reserved. No part of this publication may be reproduced or transmitted in any form or by any means, electronic or mechanical, including photocopy, recording, or any information storage and retrieval system, without the prior written permission of the publisher.

Printed in Singapore.

MJF Books and the MJF colophon are trademarks of Fine Creative Media, Inc.

TWP   10 9 8 7 6 5 4 3 2 1

DAVE RAMSEY

MONEY MATTERS

QUICK ANSWERS

TO YOUR EVERYDAY FINANCIAL QUESTIONS

MJF BOOKS
NEW YORK

TABLE OF CONTENTS

THE BASICS	9
What are the Baby Steps?	12
What counts as taxable income?	14
Does the national economy really affect my personal economy?	15
What's the most important financial principle?	16
What's the deal with debit cards and credit cards?	18
Do I need separate accounts for checking and savings?	19
DEBT, CREDIT & BANKRUPTCY	21
How do I get the ball rolling to get out of debt?	23
Why should I pay off my smallest debts first instead of starting with the highest interest rates?	24
How badly do you want to be out of debt?	26
Isn't some debt good?	28
Is it okay to buy stuff while I'm still in debt?	29
Isn't there a positive use of credit cards? Like rebates and airline miles?	30
Can debts hurt my military status?	31
Why are there so many inquiries on my credit report and what are my rights?	32
What are these strange terms on my credit report?	33
Does it help to transfer credit card debt to another card?	34
How else do the credit sharks bite?	35
I'm going to cash out my 401(k) to pay off my debts. Good idea?	36
What about debt consolidation or companies that promise to clean up my credit?	37
What about consumer credit counseling?	38
Should I sell my house to get out of debt?	39
I'm able to pay extra to my creditors. What should I do?	40
What happens to my parents' debts when they die?	41
Oops! I ran up $250,000 on credit cards. What now?	42
How should I handle collections people?	43
What can I do to stop harassment from creditors?	44
I co-signed a loan. How do I get out of it? What if that person is declaring bankruptcy?	46
Medical bills are piling up and I don't have insurance. Is bankruptcy the answer?	48
I'm trying to reestablish my credit after bankruptcy. Will a low-limit credit card help?	49
Help! My car is about to be repo'd! What should I do?	50
Help! Someone opened a credit card using my name. What should I do?	51
What is bankruptcy?	52

TABLE OF CONTENTS

RELATIONSHIPS & MONEY	55
How important is financial counseling before we get married?	57
Should I help pay my sweetie's debts before we get married?	58
Should we have joint or separate accounts?	59
Will my fiancé's bad credit affect my good rating?	60
Help! My sweetie won't kick the credit card habit! What should I do?	61
I'm deceiving my spouse about money. How can I come clean?	62
I'm better with money, but my spouse is more forceful about it. What can I do?	64
What should I do if I win the lottery?	66
My husband just left me. How do I protect my credit?	67
My spouse's spending is sinking the family. Should we call it quits?	68
We've separated and now I might be bankrupt. Should I file?	69
My ex isn't paying child support and I don't earn much. How can I make it?	70
We're trying to adopt. Should we wait to pay cash or should we borrow the money?	71
Why should we teach kids about money?	72
When should I start my kid on an allowance?	73
Why pay kids commission for things they should do anyway?	74
What's a basic way to teach children how to handle money?	75
Aren't private schools and private lessons investments into a child's future?	76
Should you ever buy a car for your child?	77
My kid won't spend her money. What should I do?	78
I'm broke and my son just moved back in. What should I do?	80
My parents are financially irresponsible. How can I help them? How can I forgive them for teaching me their bad habits?	81
BUDGETING	83
How do I get started on managing my money?	84
What are some tips for sticking to a budget?	85
What is the envelope system?	86
My income is irregular. How can I make a budget?	88
SAVING & INVESTING	91
Is saving really that important?	93
What is the secret to saving?	94
How do I get started with investing?	96
What are the basics of investing?	97

TABLE OF CONTENTS

SAVING & INVESTING (CONTINUED)

Will I retire with more money if it's invested in a Roth or a traditional IRA?	98
What types of investment plans might I be offered?	99
How do I set short-term and long-term investing goals?	100
Is a small mutual fund a good wedding gift?	102
I had a 401(k) with a company that went broke. Do I still get the money?	103
Should I cash out or roll over my 401(k)?	104
How can I invest in mutual funds with companies that align with my spiritual values?	105

20-SOMETHINGS, COLLEGE & STUDENT LOANS — 107

What are the four NEVERs of college saving?	109
How can I avoid student loans?	110
When does it make sense to go to college?	111
What are the basics on ESAs, educational IRAs, 529s, and UTMAs?	112
My son lost his scholarship. What should we do?	114
I'm a student and I'm behind on bills. What should I do?	115

STEWARDSHIP — 117

Is it acceptable to "pause" tithing in tough financial times?	118
Is it right to count my church tithes on my tax returns?	119
Should my church borrow for a new building?	120
I'm making more money now. How should I increase my giving above the tithe?	121

INSURANCE — 123

What kinds of insurance do I actually need?	125
What kind of life insurance should I get for my child and for my spouse?	126
What should I look for in good home insurance?	127

RETIREMENT & ESTATE PLANNING — 129

When is it too late to start saving for retirement?	131
Is a SEPP a good plan for the self-employed?	132
What are the best ways to save for retirement?	133
Should I pre-pay for my funeral?	134
What is a will?	135
Do I really need a will?	136
What is a living trust?	137

TABLE OF CONTENTS

AUTOMOBILES	139
Four tips for buying a vehicle.	141
Should I buy or lease a car?	142
Why buy a used car instead of a new one?	143
But I really, really, really want that car!	144
Can someone just take over the payments on a car loan?	145
How can I get out of my car lease?	146
Are extended warranties a good deal?	147
REAL ESTATE & MORTGAGES	149
Are we ready to buy a house?	150
How aggressive should I be on paying off the house?	151
Can I qualify for a mortgage with no credit?	152
Which is better—an adjustable or fixed-rate loan?	153
What are "points" and PMI?	154
What is an 80/20 mortgage and is it a good idea?	155
More Resources	156
About Dave, FPU, & the Radio Show	158

No matter what
I don't borrow money.

No matter what
I give a tenth of my income to my local
church in the Name of the Lord.

No matter what
I have an emergency fund
of three to six months of expenses.

No matter what
I don't spend over $300 without
first talking to my wife.

You've got to have some "no matter what's"
in your life.

It sounds weird doesn't it?
It used to be called common sense;
now it's a highly rated talk radio show!

THE BASICS

MONEY. We all need it, but few of us really understand it. If you listen to my daily radio show you know how desperate people are to get a handle on their finances. Maybe you're desperate . . . or maybe you're just trying to make sure you don't end up that way. Regardless, if you've picked up this book, you're interested in putting money to good use.

In *The Total Money Makeover* and my other books, I've guided people on a journey to improve their financial situations; achieving success in personal finance is a long-term process, not an overnight fix. But in *Money Matters*, I'm offering you a different approach. Instead of walking you through the chronological steps, I've created a Q&A to help you find topic-specific answers in an easy, concise format.

I only have one very simple message—be responsible to God and family, sacrifice the unnecessary to gain the necessary, get rid of debt, and build a financially peaceful future. This message is the heart of all my radio shows, articles, seminars, and books, including this one.

In *Money Matters*, it's easy to find the answers; the challenge is applying them. You see,

PERSONAL FINANCE IS 80 PERCENT BEHAVIOR AND ONLY 20 PERCENT HEAD KNOWLEDGE!

If things are going to change then YOU have to change. This isn't rocket science!

Whether you are selling something or whether you want to gain control of your personal finances . . . it's all about behavior adjustments. You can't walk through the mall if you have a spending problem—it's like a drunk hanging out at a bar.

So, get on with it. Your future awaits the decisions you make today!

TOP TWO WAYS TO BE MONEY $MART

1. Say "no" to credit cards.
2. Write it down. Make a budget. Give every dollar a name.

WHAT ARE THE BABY STEPS?

L eaping financial hurdles doesn't come easy or immediately. First you have to get your balance and learn to walk. Here are the Baby Steps.

1. $1,000 in an Emergency Fund
2. Pay off all debt (except the house) utilizing the "Debt Snowball"
3. Three to six months expenses in savings for emergencies
4. Fully fund 15 percent into pre-tax retirement plans and ROTH IRA, if eligible
5. College funding
6. Pay off home early
7. Build wealth! (Mutual funds and real estate)

MONEY ACTION

I'm on Baby Step #
_____

I've been on this Step since
_____

_____

_____

I want to get to the next Step by
_____

_____

_____

_____

_____

Believe you can do this!

WHAT COUNTS AS TAXABLE INCOME?

Among the things that typically count as income are:
- Anything from your employer
- Tips
- Odd jobs
- Interest
- Profit on sale of stocks and other investments
- Profit on sale of property
- Alimony
- Social Security
- Some retirement savings
- Settlements from lawsuits
- Lottery or gambling winnings

Among the things that usually don't count as income are:
- Scholarships
- Inherited money (the estate already paid taxes on this)
- Life insurance payouts

DOES THE NATIONAL ECONOMY REALLY AFFECT MY PERSONAL ECONOMY?

The news keeps telling us about the unemployment rate and jobs being lost. We hear about economic indicators that affect the stock market. When the government is concerned about the economy, it lowers interest rates in an effort to keep people spending. Debt is rising.

So what is the truth? News reporters don't give the full truth. They bring the bleeding stories to us to get the ratings. Hardly ever do you hear positive news as a lead story.

The truth is that all those economic factors do affect you, but what you do in your own home will affect you far more.

The reality is that some people have lost jobs, but the beauty of the Baby Steps is that the system works both in good times and in bad times. It is God's and Grandma's way of handling money. Debt-free living on a plan (a budget), saving for emergencies, investing for long-term goals, living on less than you make, and agreeing with your spouse on spending makes you prosperous—not tomorrow, but over time. Getting rich quick doesn't work.

Wake up—you'd better start to prosper now! This is the best economy ever. If you cannot build wealth now, when can you build wealth? Get to work now!

WHAT'S THE MOST IMPORTANT FINANCIAL PRINCIPLE? (THE ANSWER MIGHT SURPRISE YOU.)

The *Dave Ramsey Show* and my company, the Lampo Group, have become very well known for teaching people how to get out of debt, save money, and get on a budget. All of us on staff here are very thankful for the response we've had to these concepts, but another financial concept is the hinge on which the door of successful personal finance swings. I have only begun to realize the full significance of this concept during the last year or so. When you understand this concept, all the other concepts work, and until you implement it, none of them will work. When you stick this concept deep in your soul, it becomes easy to save money, and even have money to invest. Getting out of debt happens quickly once you learn how to apply this concept in your life. Budgeting is made easier and your marriage or relationships regarding money are freed up and made smooth. This is the most important financial concept.

Contentment. That's right, contentment. Contentment brings peace. Not apathy. Not the deadhead fog of Prozac or Valium. Only contentment brings peace. We live in the most marketed-to society in the history of the world, and the very essence of marketing is to disturb your peace. We say things to ourselves like, "I'll be happy when I get that boat;" or I'll be happy when I get that china cabinet;" or "I'll be happy when I get that house." Or, or, or, or!!!

NOT TRUE. Happiness is sold to us as an event or a thing, and consequently, our finances have suffered. Fun can be bought with money, but happiness cannot.

We live among a bunch of people who are deeply in debt and have no money saved because their emotions were tricked. Just like drug addicts, people have been conned into believing that happiness will come with the next purchase. So, Daddy works hundreds of overtime hours and Mommy works forty–plus hours a week, all in the name of STUFF.

You probably think I am writing about someone else, but I'm not. I am writing about you. I know because I suffer from the same disease—but I am recovering and so are many of you. The human spirit was not created to attain peace, contentment, or fulfillment by gathering more stuff.

You can get out of debt, save money, and get on a budget, but until your intellect forces your emotions and your spirit to accept that STUFF does not equal CONTENTMENT, your finances will always feel stressed. At our office we counsel every week with folks who are making $25,000 per year as well as folks making $250,000 per year. These people share a common problem: they all suffer from some level of "stuffitis," the worship of stuff. Change your focus and change your life for the better.

WHAT'S THE DEAL WITH DEBIT CARDS AND CREDIT CARDS?

A debit card looks like a credit card. It may have the same logos as a credit card, and most places will let you use it just like a credit card. But it's not a credit card.

The main difference is that when you use a debit card, the money comes directly out of your account, instead of coming from the credit card company for you to pay back later with interest. You're spending money you already have, not money you hope you'll have.

The danger in using a debit card is that you are still using plastic, which takes the emotion out of spending. For day-to-day purchases, I still recommend using cash because it hurts more to let it go.

If you lose your debit card—call the card issuer and report the loss immediately. If unauthorized use occurs before you report it, the amount you can be held liable for depends upon how quickly you report the loss. For instance, if you report the loss within two business days you will not be responsible for more than $50 for unauthorized use.

If you lose your credit card—call and cancel it immediately. You don't need a replacement. Consider the loss a good opportunity to stop feeding the credit shark, although you may be liable for fees for any unauthorized use.

A better idea is not to wait until you lose your credit card; cancel it today.

DO I NEED SEPARATE ACCOUNTS FOR CHECKING AND SAVINGS?

You definitely need to separate your checking and savings accounts. This is especially important when it comes to your emergency fund. It is so easy to write a check that dips into your emergency fund, which will defeat the original purpose. The separation is a mental note to yourself that you've reached your spending boundary.

But your savings account does need to have check writing privileges, just in case you need that emergency fund to cover an emergency.

If you want to learn about success, listen to someone who has succeeded.
H. W. ARNOLD

God gives every bird its food,
but He does not throw it into the nest.

J. G. HOLLAND

The haves and have–nots
can often be traced back to the dids
and the did–nots.

D. O. FLYNN

DEBT, CREDIT & BANKRUPTCY

DEBT is dumb. Most normal people are just plain broke because they are in debt up to their eyeballs. The Bible says, "The borrower is servant to the lender." If you're in debt then you're a slave; you do not have the freedom to use your money to powerfully change your family tree.

Debt is normal! So why be normal? Do you want to be like 70 percent of all households that live paycheck to paycheck? It takes a lot of will, discipline, and courage to slay the debt monster. But it can be done. Think—how much could you put toward retirement if you didn't have a car payment?

The concept of credit itself is "new" to the personal finance scene. What? Yes, that's right. The idea of using credit as a significant aspect of one's personal financial plan is less than fifty years old. After the 1950s, credit became a marketing tool by companies that wanted to convince consumers to buy even affordable items on credit. The message of credit is, "Enjoy now and pay for it later."

The average household gets six new credit card offers every month, and the average college student gets one new offer every few days! Some people are more protective of their credit rating than of any other thing, when credit is the monster that's destroying their future and sending them down the road to bankruptcy. Even the sound of that word sends chills up the spine. But if you're facing the prospect of bankruptcy, or if you're in the middle of it right now, it's a living nightmare. It's scary. It can devastate your job and your marriage.

The first thing you need to know is that you can make it. I was there personally at age 24. I lost it all. I know the shame, the pain, the hurt, the fear, and all the other emotions that come with bankruptcy. There really is hope.

If you are considering bankruptcy you also need to know that I recommend bankruptcy about as often as I recommend divorce—almost never! There are options most people have never examined that could actually prevent bankruptcy.

Debt is dumb, and credit destroys. But you don't have to fall into the traps. Welcome to the real world!

HOW DO I GET THE BALL ROLLING TO GET OUT OF DEBT?

We've developed a little process called the "Baby Steps" to do one thing at a time and keep it simple. The principle is to stop everything except minimum payments, and focus on one thing at a time. Otherwise nothing gets accomplished because all your effort is diluted.

First accumulate $1,000 cash as an emergency fund. Then begin intensely getting rid of all debt (except the house) using the debt snowball. You attack the smallest debt first, still maintaining minimum payments on everything else. Do what is necessary to focus your attention. Keep stepping up to next larger bill.

After the credit debt is taken care of, work to build the emergency fund up to three to six months of expenses.

Now start putting fifteen percent of your income into retirement funds. Then save for your kids' college expenses, and then go to work on paying off the house. Once that is finished, investing is very easy to do. It's all just a matter of doing it.

I have been broke. I know how scared I felt, and I know how fast I wanted to get away from debt. I know how you feel, and I have learned that what really works is unbelievably fierce, focused intensity.

WHY SHOULD I PAY OFF MY SMALLEST DEBTS FIRST INSTEAD OF STARTING WITH THE HIGHEST INTEREST RATES?

The math seems to lean more toward paying the highest interest debts first, but what I have learned is that personal finance is 20 percent head knowledge and 80 percent behavior. You need some quick wins in order to stay pumped enough to get completely out of debt. When you start knocking off the easier debts, you will start to see results and you will start to win.

You don't drown by falling in the water, you drown by staying there.
EDWIN LOUIS COLE

THE DEBT SNOWBALL

List all your debts from smallest to largest. Start working the snowball and watch your victories grow!

DEBT OWED	CREDITOR	MINIMUM PAYMENT	DATE PAID OFF
$300	Big Store	$25	JAN. 21, 2005
$8,483	Visa	$200	AUG. 2, 2005
$17,850	Dealership	$400	SELL CAR

HOW BADLY DO YOU WANT TO BE OUT OF DEBT?

Many hard-working people get into debt because of mistakes. I work with those people every day. I'm talking about them—those who are willing to keep working hard—when I promise that there's hope for a financially peaceful future.

But then there are lazy people. Laziness is a character flaw. You need to be willing to work in order to fix the situations that you created with your own irresponsibility. If you are not willing, then you cannot be helped.

Are you willing to get another job and work a few 80-hour weeks? If you are in financial stress because of something you've done, you need to get yourself out of the mess by working. If you think that is too hard, you will never get out of the debt that you brought upon yourself. Laziness is a sickness, and it will get you absolutely nowhere in life. We all make mistakes, but the question is whether you are willing to take responsibility for your mistakes! You need to learn from your mistakes or you—and your children—will be doomed to repeat the cycle.

How badly do you want to be out of debt?

You're not stuck where you are unless you decide to be.
WAYNE DYER

Getting out of debt takes getting mad.
It takes the willingness to
live off rice and beans for a while.
It takes getting a second or third job
and selling stuff.
If you really want to get out of debt,
this is what you will do.
It's called "getting mad."

ISN'T SOME DEBT GOOD?

Some financial advisers, economists, columnists and other so-called experts keep saying that some loans are necessary, or that living without any debt at all is just plain impractical. These people believe that you receive great benefits by going into debt.

Give me a break! These guys are idiots. What's more, they're probably broke idiots. Do you want to take money advice from broke people? No!

You are not "simple" or "emotional" if you believe in being debt-free. What we have been taught about "good debt" is what brings us to the pathetic financial state that this economy is in.

The only good debt is debt that is paid off.

Debt is normal. But the truth is that you should not want to be normal. You need to be willing to be weird. Weird is when you live sacrificially in the present, pay off your past, and invest in a financially peaceful future.

IS IT OKAY TO BUY STUFF WHILE I'M STILL IN DEBT?

I recommend waiting. Sometimes things are necessities, but most things are not. If you want to purchase a leather couch, you should wait until you pay off all your debts. The couch is not something you need. Being out of debt so that your family can live and save is more important than buying the leather couch. I look at priorities. As long as you have what you need to physically survive, very few things are more important than getting out of debt as quickly as possible.

Sometimes people borrow money to pay off debt, and they just go deeper and deeper into debt. When you have more money going out than there is coming in, you are simply borrowing to pay your bills.

This is the point where you need to take the bull by the horns. You need to be sacrificial, crazy, and you need to make some painful decisions. You need to sell the car, the house, have a garage sale, and so forth. These are not pleasant things, but you need to make these decisions yourself or someone will make them for you.

ISN'T THERE A POSITIVE USE OF CREDIT CARDS? LIKE REBATES AND AIRLINE MILES?

Responsible use of credit cards does not exist. There is NO positive side to credit card use. You WILL spend more if you use credit cards. Even by paying the bills on time, you are not beating the system! You are falling for a lie.

Think about the rebates. If you were using a credit card at 5 percent, you would have had to have spent $160,000 to get $4,000 rebates on new cars that lost $6,000 of value when you drove them off the lot. That is not a good deal.

When you pay in cash, you can "feel" the money leaving you. This is not true with credit cards. Flipping a card up on a counter registers nothing emotionally. If you use plastic instead of cash you will spend 12 percent to 18 percent more. This is money you could have saved.

If you "have to" use plastic, I suggest VISA debit cards. I use them for travel and the occasional convenience of ordering something over the Internet or phone. Other than that, I use cash.

Personal finance is 80 percent behavior. You need to cut out habits that make you spend more. You do not build wealth with credit cards. Use common sense. When you play with a multi-billion dollar industry and you think you're going to win at their game, you are naïve. You cannot beat the credit card companies.

CAN DEBTS HURT MY MILITARY STATUS?

It is possible to get a dishonorable discharge because of financial irresponsibility. This is the third largest reason for discharge in the military today. But if you continue to earnestly work on paying off your debt, you do not have to worry about being discharged because of your financial situation.

Anything that you legally signed for, you need to take responsibility for and pay off.

If you're deployed overseas, then based upon the Soldiers' and Sailors' Civil Relief Act, anything you did not legally sign for can wait until you get home from deployment.

Your creditors can't really do anything in the meantime; they are not going to bring you home over a car repo!

Maturity doesn't come with age; it comes with acceptance of responsibility.
ED COLE

WHY ARE THERE SO MANY INQUIRIES ON MY CREDIT REPORT AND WHAT ARE MY RIGHTS?

Under the Federal Fair Credit Reporting Act, anyone with a valid business reason can get a copy of your credit report with or without your permission. That even includes when you apply for a job.

What you see on your report are marketing inquiries. That's why you keep getting credit card and home equity loan offers in the mailbox. You can put a block on your bureau that would prohibit unsolicited marketing inquiries.

Our society has become so debt-ridden that many people find themselves worshiping at the altar of the credit bureau. You need to know that there are laws set up for you, and you have certain rights when communicating with your bureau.

You have the right to obtain your credit report, and the bureau has the right to charge you for it. If you have been turned down by a bank or place of employment as a result of your credit report, you are entitled to a free copy upon the delivery of a refusal letter.

You have the right to dispute inaccurate information on your credit report. The credit bureau has thirty days by law to fix the report if you are correct.

See page 157 for how to contact credit reporting agencies.

WHAT ARE THESE STRANGE TERMS ON MY CREDIT REPORT?

If you were offered a "paid charge off," this means there was an amount you owed, but the lender forgave the debt under the circumstances. This is a gray mark on your credit report.

"Paid collection" means you did not have the money, but the leasing company agreed to accept nothing. If a lender agrees to completely drop your debt for you, you need to be sure to get it in writing.

If you settled a credit card debt for less than the amount, your credit card report will read "settled in full." This means exactly what it says, and you need to require it as a part of what you get in writing when you settle. People can look at your report and see that you did not pay all your debt, but you did pay all your settlement. It is a gray mark on your report. It is not a positive thing, but it will allow you to get a house later.

Another variation that shows up on credit reports is "paid in full, not full price." This is not a black mark on your credit report, but it does not mean you are totally clean either. Basically, it means that you got in a little mess, but pulled yourself out of it honorably.

DOES IT HELP TO TRANSFER CREDIT CARD DEBT TO ANOTHER CARD?

Sometimes it helps to transfer credit debt to another credit card that has a lower interest rate. This certainly will save you interest. The only problem is that you might feel like you have done something and get lazy on paying off your debt.

Switching to a lower interest rate is okay, but it is only about 2 percent of the plan. The other 98 percent is you getting insane and attacking this debt of yours. The $100 you are going to save in interest is not the problem; your $2,500 debt is the problem.

The German root word for "debt" is the same as for "guilt."

HOW ELSE DO THE CREDIT SHARKS BITE?

Credit sharks use all sorts of tactics as they circle their prey—you—but they can't move in for the feeding frenzy until you slip up. Here are some of the things they offer:

0% interest plans—You cannot afford to lose money. This 0 percent does not save you money, especially when you are talking about automobiles that drop in value like a rock. Stay away from 0 percent financing no matter where it is—it's all designed to get you into the stores. It's NOT a good deal.

e–duction—This allows your monthly payment to be deducted directly from your paycheck, but the bottom line is that you are spending what you have not yet earned. You will literally be working for the credit card company! Wake up and don't be stupid. This is not a good idea.

"Pre–loaded" cards—These are similar to pre–paid phone cards or gift cards in that they have a certain amount of money on it that a consumer can spend. Then, the cards can be reloaded with more money when it runs out. These are NOT helpful for teaching kids how to use money—they're just teaching kids how to use plastic. Did you ever think about keeping your kids OUT of debt? How about letting your kid carry cash around? These cards are a bad idea. They do not teach students how to be financially responsible; they teach them how to get into debt.

I'M GOING TO CASH OUT MY 401(K) TO PAY OFF MY DEBTS. GOOD IDEA?

Wait a minute. You're cashing out your 401(k) to pay off debts? NO! You will be taxed 40 percent on the cash out. That is equivalent to taking a loan out at 40 percent interest. You have sixty days to reinvest your money, which can be done by calling your employer's human resources department.

I rarely recommend cashing out your 401(k). But if it looks like you cannot survive without paying off the debt, you'll need to set aside money for taxes. Don't touch a dime of it. Put yourself on a strict budget to avoid another big mess.

Now, about your debt.

Say that the total debt is around $8,000, while your 401(k) is $12,000. You or your spouse could deliver pizzas to pay $1,000 a month, so you could be debt-free in eight months and still have your retirement. That $12,000 invested would amount to $431,000 in thirty years.

Cashing out this money now could end up being a $500,000 mistake.

WHAT ABOUT DEBT CONSOLIDATION OR COMPANIES THAT PROMISE TO CLEAN UP MY CREDIT?

Debt CONsolidation doesn't work. You end up paying about the same amount. The truth is that you cannot borrow your way out of debt!!!

The way you get out of debt is by changing your habits. You need to commit to get on a written game plan—a budget—and stick to it. Get an extra job and start paying off the debt. Live on less than you make. It is not rocket science.

You've probably seen the commercials for companies that claim they can clean up your credit for you. Don't go there. There are two basic problems with them.

1—For purposes of getting a mortgage, going through companies that take your money and pay your bills will reflect on your credit as if you filed a chapter 13 bankruptcy.

2—Only transactions seven years or older, or a mistake, may be taken off your credit report. A company that says otherwise is either lying or operating illegally.

WHAT ABOUT CONSUMER CREDIT COUNSELING?

There are three components to my opinion.

1—They do a great job if you have lots of credit card debt.
2—For purposes of getting a mortgage, it shows on your credit report as if you filed bankruptcy.
3—They don't address the problem of spending too much.

You can develop a payment plan on your own. Consumer Credit Counseling Service cannot teach you to manage money, which is what you need to learn. Only then will the cycle of debt be stopped for you and your family.

A real solution is to take an extra job that is flexible to supplement your other income. You can also call the credit card companies to negotiate the interest rates on your cards. Tell them you are going to transfer the balance to another card with a lower interest rate. This usually works and gets them to lower your rate. Just remember to not borrow your way out of debt.

SHOULD I SELL MY HOUSE TO GET OUT OF DEBT?

If your payment is more than 45 percent of your take-home pay, the numbers will sink you. You should consider selling unless you see a large increase in income on the near horizon.

But most of the time, if the only reason to sell the house is to get out of debt, don't do it. Just attack the debt. I very rarely recommend selling your personal residence simply to get out of debt.

But if you have other reasons for selling, this might be a good plan.

Being mediocre, and just living check to check, worry to worry, problem to problem all your whole life—that's the hard stuff. The easy stuff is sacrificing, focusing, and being intense for just a few years. It will be worth it.

I'M ABLE TO PAY EXTRA TO CREDITORS. WHAT SHOULD I DO?

Congratulations on making progress.

When you're making extra payments, the first thing to do is to make sure that the extra money goes directly toward paying off the principal. You don't want to just pay on the interest.

I suggest that if there isn't a line on the bill to put X number of dollars extra towards principal, write an extra check in a separate envelope and write "principal only" on the check.

Also, verify with your creditor to find out whether there's a fee for paying off a bill early. You may be able to negotiate out of it.

If your creditor refuses to apply the extra money directly to the principal, call every day to complain until they do.

Those who work hard will make a profit, but those who only talk will be poor.
PROVERBS 14:23 NCV

WHAT HAPPENS TO MY PARENTS' DEBTS AFTER THEY DIE?

Any outstanding debt that your parents will have upon their passing will go against their estate. The home may be sold by the executor of the estate in order to pay their debts. The things they owe will be placed against the things they own. If there is a positive net worth, meaning there is more money once the debts are paid off, you will get this as an inheritance. If there is a negative net worth, meaning once everything was sold they still owe, you will not be held liable for these debts.

You are not responsible for paying off the debts of your parents after they die. You are not even responsible for your deceased spouse's debts, including student loans. However, the entire estate would have to be liquidated and paid against the debts before anything is left to the heirs. If an entire estate is liquidated and there is still outstanding debt, the creditors just eat it and the debt disappears.

To avoid this, people with any debt need to get on a really tight budget. Make a game plan for handling finances so that in the event of death, the bereaved will be left with property, not a mess.

Also, keep in mind that $10,000 to $15,000 will be needed to cover the funerals and burials of two people in most states. It's painful, but you need to think about this.

OOPS! I RAN UP $250,000 ON CREDIT CARDS. WHAT NOW?

You'd be surprised at how many people owe $100,000 or more on credit cards. That's bad news. But you can do something about it without declaring bankruptcy.

Say you're making $60,000 a year. If you live on $30,000, you can get this debt gone in eight years. If you have some equity in a house, sell it.

You need to do some extra things to increase your income, and I'm not talking about day trading or some get-rich-quick scheme. You can work your way out of this. You're going to live on nothing to get out of this.

If you've missed a lot of payments, it's likely that you'll be offered settlements to pay back just pennies on the actual dollars you owe. You're broke and so the creditors are going to be thrilled to get any money at all. You are a bankruptcy waiting to happen as far as they are concerned.

The only time I'd consider debt consolidation is for taking advantage of settlements. Just remember that if you take those consolidation loans, you still have to pay on those. This stuff will stay on your credit report for seven years after the last activity.

You can get out of this mess; you just have to live sacrificially and work at it.

HOW SHOULD I HANDLE COLLECTIONS PEOPLE?

Not all collectors are bad; several of them are just doing their job. People with credit debt owe money, so collectors call to ask for it. There is nothing wrong with that. If a company calls and wants to know when they are getting paid, you need to talk them. Don't just hang up on them unless they're being rude or harassing.

But a lot of collectors break the law on a daily basis. Collectors' only concern is to get the money, not help you. Remember, collectors go through little training and are not paid very much. The industry has a high turnover rate; it's tough to be a professional bully.

Collectors are trained to make people emotional on the phone. If they can get you angry, upset, or crying, you are more likely to pay them than pay your landlord. They yell, scream, threaten, and intimidate. Fourteen phone calls a night is illegal, but it's also a reality.

I am not teaching you to dodge your creditors or not pay your bills, but long conversations on the phone with these people will cause you to fold. Short, simple conversations informing the creditor of where you are in your payment is as long as the conversation needs to be.

Do not let them convince you to pay your bills out of order—survival necessities first, then creditors. You've got to stay in control of the situation.

WHAT CAN I DO TO STOP HARASSMENT FROM CREDITORS?

You owe what you owe. I'm not telling you to get out of paying your debts. But if your creditors are going overboard, you need to get those lunatics under control.

The best place to go if collectors are over the top is the Federal Trade Commission, but be sure you follow through.

If you've asked a creditor to stop calling you at your workplace, you need to overnight a letter to the person harassing you and to the company headquarters. Send two letters and get proof of delivery with a tracking number from FedEx or UPS. You need to say, "Our financial counselor has informed us you are breaking federal law. According to the Federal Fair Debt Collections Act, once you have been notified not to call an office, you are required to never call back again. Please call back one more time, because I would love to own your company! I will sue you and report you to every agency if you call me at work again!" You must have this physical proof in case this does go to court. You can't just call because people will lie.

If a creditor is harassing you about someone else's debt, like for a friend or relative who might have used your phone number, you need to record the phone conversation the next time they call. Tell the creditor that what they are doing is illegal, that if they call again you are going to sue for a huge sum of money and file a complaint with the Federal Trade Commission. Tell the creditor that you are recording the conversation to use in court, then hire an attorney because they are violating federal law. You're dealing with a moron in a cubicle 500 miles away, and you have to treat them that way.

If a creditor is threatening to garnish your wages or sue you, stay calm. If you have a low balance, a creditor probably won't sue you because a lawsuit costs more than your balance on the card. Because creditors understand that, they have to use other methods of collection, like intimidation. These methods more often are to evoke emotion such as anger and fear. I suggest you:

• Make sure you have caller ID to screen calls. You only need to be in contact with collectors every two weeks.

• Get an answering machine with a Memo button so you can record those harassing calls.

• Send a written budget and show them how much you can pay them each month. Send only that amount and then when you have more, send more.

Never pay electronically, over the phone, or using post–dated checks! Instead, overnight a check to the right address.

I CO-SIGNED ON A LOAN. HOW DO I GET OUT OF IT? WHAT IF THAT PERSON IS DECLARING BANKRUPTCY?

You signed a note of responsibility when you co-signed on the loan. But now you need your name off that loan in order to fix your own credit.

The best bet may be to have the primary signer of the loan re-finance it with someone else as the co-signer. The quicker you get out of the loan, the quicker your credit can be repaired.

If the primary signer is going bankrupt, refinancing probably won't be an option.

If the other person on the loan has filed bankruptcy, it should not show up on your credit report that YOU filed bankruptcy, but it will show up that the note was bankrupted on.

Remember—the purpose of a co-signer is to guarantee the loan. If they don't pay, you do!

Ignoring a problem just makes it get bigger. When you don't pay something you owe, it accumulates collection fees & penalties. These extra fees are called **stupid tax** for waiting around instead of taking care of a problem. Find a way to pay what you owe.

MEDICAL BILLS ARE PILING UP, AND I DON'T HAVE INSURANCE. IS BANKRUPTCY THE ANSWER?

There is no magic pill. Fortunately, medical bills are the most flexible as far as settling terms and working out for cash when there isn't insurance.

I suggest you go to the hospital with your financial situation laid out, and ask them for help in setting up a payment plan. They usually will work with you when you meet with them face to face.

Don't file bankruptcy. You're going to be able to settle.

The worst bankruptcy in the world is the person who has lost their enthusiasm. Let someone lose everything else in the world but their enthusiasm and they will come through again to success.

H. W. ARNOLD

I'M TRYING TO REESTABLISH MY CREDIT AFTER BANKRUPTCY. WILL A LOW-LIMIT CREDIT CARD HELP?

NO! That's a terrible idea! After bankruptcy, all creditors are your best friends, because they know you cannot declare again on them!

Why do people file Chapter 7 anyway? Because they are too far in debt. So why, as soon as you get out, do you want to get back in debt again! Isn't that something to avoid!

You do not need to re-establish your credit. Why would you want to re-establish your credit? So later on you can go out and get in debt again?

Do you know what avoiding credit cards for three to five years shows a mortgage lender? Wisdom! It shows you got it! It shows that you know what debt can do to you. That is the kind of person a mortgage lender is looking for, not someone who declared bankruptcy and then got more credit cards again!

You do not need a big hairy credit report to buy things and survive in America.

HELP! MY CAR IS ABOUT TO BE REPO'D! WHAT SHOULD I DO?

There is no sure-fire solution. The bank may be willing to compromise about the missed car payments. If they are, make sure it is in writing; otherwise the original contract still stands. A deal may buy two weeks of time.

But the repossession is a symptom of the real problem—you're outspending your income. Serious changes are needed to turn this issue around. Your first responsibility is not the pursuit of your own personal happiness; it is to feed your family.

Failure is the opportunity to begin again more intelligently.
HENRY FORD

HELP! SOMEONE OPENED A CREDIT CARD USING MY NAME! WHAT SHOULD I DO?

You need to put a fraud victim alert on your credit report immediately. You also need to file a police report and possibly have the person who did this arrested for criminal fraud.

When dealing with the credit card companies, talk to the fraud victim division and be sure they do not convince you to pay. You did not run up these bills, a criminal did, and you should not pay a dime.

Man must work. That is certain as the sun. But we may work grudgingly or he may work gratefully... There is no work so rude, that he may not exalt it; no work so impassive, that he may not breathe a soul into it; no work so dull that he may not enliven it.
HENRY GILES

WHAT IS BANKRUPTCY?

Bankruptcy is a process established by a set of federal laws that is designed to give debtors a "fresh start" by canceling many of their debts through an order of the court. Bankruptcy also allows creditors a chance to get their designated shares of any money the debtors can afford to, or are obligated to, pay back.

When a bankruptcy is filed, creditors have to stop any attempt to collect a debt, at least temporarily. There is usually immediate relief from creditor pressure, and a bankruptcy can stop a pending foreclosure sale of your home, a garnishment of your wages, or a threatened repossession. Most creditors cannot call, write, or sue you after you have filed bankruptcy.

For specific bankruptcy information based on your city of residence visit CityLegalGuide.com.

Personal bankruptcy usually does not erase child support, alimony, fines, taxes, and some student loan obligations. Also, unless you have an acceptable plan to catch up on your debt under Chapter 13, bankruptcy usually does not allow you to keep property when your creditor has an unpaid mortgage or lien on it.

MONEY ACTION

When things were not looking good for Sharon and me, we would pull out our "Hope Sheet." Anytime we would achieve a goal or do something good, we would write it down on the list. Whenever we would feel like things were hopeless, we would pull out the "hope Sheet" and read how far we had come. It is always good to reflect and remind ourselves of how much we have achieved when times seem dark.

MY HOPE SHEET

SUCCESS	DATE
GOT MAD (MOTIVATED ABOUT DEBT)	10/14/04
PAID CASH FOR CHRISTMAS PRESENTS	12/21/04

Opposites attract.
If two people just alike get
married, one of you
is unnecessary.

LARRY BURKETT

RELATIONSHIPS & MONEY

OPPOSITES ATTRACT. So what does that mean? It means that chances are that if you're married, one of you is good at working numbers (the nerd) and the other one isn't good at working numbers (the free spirit). That isn't the real problem. The problem is when the nerd neglects the input of the free spirit, or when the free spirit avoids participating in the financial dealings altogether.

Marriage is a partnership. The preacher said, "And now you are one." Both parties need to be involved in the finances. Separating the finances and splitting the bills is a bad idea.

Listen up, nerds. Don't keep the finances all to yourself. And don't use your "power" to abuse the free spirit.

Free spirits, don't just nod your head and say, "Yeah, that looks great, honey." You have a vote, too, in the budget committee meetings.

Give feedback, criticism, and encouragement. Work on the budget together!

"But what if my spouse won't get on board with me?" many of you wonder. It is tough, but with patience and kindness (don't beat them over the head with the need for a budget and please don't subject your spouse to a lecture of "Dave Says") your spouse will eventually see the light.

As you work on your finances together, you will begin to change your family tree. One of your main goals in your marriage should be to pass a legacy down to your children and grandchildren. If you want that legacy to be a blessing and not a curse, though, you need to teach your kids how to handle money.

It is never too early to start teaching your kids about money. And the earlier you start them, the better their good saving, spending, and giving habits will develop.

One of the most important things you can do is to teach the value and reward of work. I recommend paying "commissions" for chores. The goal isn't to turn your children into union negotiators, but you also don't want to teach them to take a free ride. As your children (younger and older) earn money, you need to help them learn to live on a plan—a budget. Help them create an envelope system and teach them to save some, give some, and spend some.

Take advantage of every opportunity you come across to teach your children financial wisdom.

HOW IMPORTANT IS FINANCIAL COUNSELING BEFORE WE GET MARRIED?

There are four areas where you should be in agreement before you get married. This will tremendously increase your chances of surviving as a couple. The four areas are religion, children, parents, and money.

As an engagement gift, you could go through Financial Peace University together. Or read through *The Total Money Makeover* together. Do something to unify your financial head–knowledge, so you can begin your marriage with smart financial behaviors.

If you can't find ways to agree about how to handle money, I suggest that you put the marriage off until you are of the same accord.

But when you come into unity on this subject it creates romance. It creates communication about the most important things in your life between yourself and your spouse.

Also, never marry someone who insists on a prenuptial agreement. Some people think these are just insurance in case the marriage sours; others say it's like planning a divorce. As difficult as it might be, I'd recommend that you postpone or cancel your wedding to someone who wants a prenuptial agreement. Do not marry someone who loves their money more than they love you.

SHOULD I HELP PAY MY SWEETIE'S DEBTS BEFORE WE GET MARRIED?

Why would you help pay those debts now? You're not married yet. Those bills will become your joint responsibility once you are married and not a minute earlier.

What is your responsibility now is making sure that you agree on financial issues before you say the big "I do." This does not mean that you need to be debt free to get married, but you should certainly be in agreement before you get married regarding financial spending and lifestyle.

This person you are engaged to will have to deal with their financial issues. Dealing with debt is not only a mental thing, it is also emotional. You need to get in control of the situation before you get married. The number one reason for divorce is because of disputes about money. Solve that problem now and your marriage will have a chance.

SHOULD WE HAVE JOINT OR SEPARATE ACCOUNTS?

I do not think that you should have separate accounts for your personal finances. You are a team. Work together. You and your spouse should keep your personal finances in one account, paying and spending everything together.

When you are separating yourselves in marriage, you are setting yourselves up for divorce! When you get married, you are together forever, and that means with money, assets, and finances as well.

I do think that you should separate your personal finances from your business finances, if you have a business. This makes accounting easier.

Keep your lives free from the love of money and be content with what you have, because God has said, "Never will I leave you; never will I forsake you."
HEBREWS 13:5 NIV

WILL MY FIANCÉ'S BAD CREDIT AFFECT MY GOOD RATING?

Bad credit does not leap off of your husband's or wife's credit report over onto yours just because you put a ring on your finger. Your individual credit report will be fine.

Where it will affect you is when you try to purchase things together in the future. When you want to purchase a home, you will face difficulty, because it will involve his bad credit. Make sure you don't go out and put everything under your name either!

A good wedding present for you two would be to go through a 13-week series from Financial Peace University. I wish someone had taught me the stuff I know now when I had first gotten married!

HELP! MY SWEETIE WON'T KICK THE CREDIT CARD HABIT! WHAT CAN I DO?

This is a behavior thing, and behaviors always include emotions. Ask yourself, "What is the advantage in his/her mind of using a credit card?"

Is it convenience? A debit card can do that.

Is it for emergencies? A debit card can do that.

Is it to buy things you can't afford? Hmmmm.

The best thing for the two of you is to sit down and decide together that you are going to start using debit cards instead of credit cards because you want things under control. Then start tackling any credit card debts.

Many a man has failed because he had his wishbone where his backbone should have been.
RONALD REAGAN

I'M DECEIVING MY SPOUSE ABOUT MONEY. HOW CAN I COME CLEAN?

The most pressure-filled issue that comes up when counseling is broken trust in marital communication in money matters. Time and time again, I see the pain and tears that come from one spouse who has attempted to hide or fix (unsuccessfully) an uncontrolled spending habit. Sometimes it's the man and sometimes it's the woman. The pressure is real and must be met with compassion and tough love.

The balance between caring and supporting the person and holding them accountable is learned by experience and commitment. Everyone is susceptible to impulsive, unscheduled purchases, but when they become uncontrollable it is difficult to admit to them. This happens when a husband wants to know how to hide from his wife the fact that he has spent $15,000 on credit cards. Or when a wife wants to know how to pay off $12,000 in credit cards her husband doesn't know about. This addictive behavior is occurring regularly. (If you are the unsuspecting spouse, respond with compassion and forgiveness.)

Let's explore some basic baby steps to recovery:

1. Make sure you prepare to tell the whole truth. This is half the battle in taking responsibility for your actions.

2. Set a time to sit down with your spouse, asking them not to respond until you have completed making your confession, and then tell them, as honestly as you can, exactly what has happened. This time should include asking their forgiveness. Be prepared prayerfully for any potential

response, because this may be quite a shock to your spouse.

3. Ask them to tell you how they are feeling and listen attentively without responding, even if there is silence.

4. Ask your spouse to help you work out a plan to attack the debt using the snowball or selling an item even if at a loss.

5. Establish a time, weekly at first, to stay accountable with each other to curb any relapse of your behavior. If there is a relapse, it may be time to see a counselor for some additional guidance.

6. When the crisis is over and wounds have healed, continue to seek your spouse's counsel. It may seem obvious, but couples too often make big financial decisions without talking first. It is important to agree about major purchases, even if they are in your budget. Talking before either of you acts will help you make better decisions, build unity in your marriage, and help return the peace and trust to your relationship.

Whatever motivated the behavior, the goal is to own up to it and begin taking specific steps to replace the habit. The journey is not an easy one, but worth every step. Peace will result.

Be kind and compassionate to one another, forgiving each other, just as in Christ, God forgave you.
Ephesians 4:32

I'M BETTER WITH MONEY, BUT MY SPOUSE IS MORE FORCEFUL ABOUT IT. WHAT CAN I DO?

In most marriages, one person is more forceful than the other. If the forceful one isn't wise, guess what happens? A lot of stupid decisions are made for the family!

Those of you who are NOT the forceful ones in marriages must speak out when you think a decision is wrong! Do not go along with stupidity. If you know what is right, grow a backbone and speak up!

Relationships play a huge role in your ability to win in the wealth-building game. If the wiser person in the marriage is also the less assertive, then stupid things are always going to be done unless the wiser one learns to stand up to the forceful one.

Those of you who aren't forceful, you need to grow a spine for your family's good. You need to learn to say "no" to stupid decisions. You don't have to be nasty, but you do have to be assertive. The first time you do this there may be a fight. You may need some counseling. But you needed it anyway—if stupidity is what keeps the boat stable, you are sailing right into a hurricane. Don't put off the pain anymore, because it is coming.

For your own good, for the good of your family and your future, grow a backbone. When something is wrong, stand up and say it is wrong, and don't back down.

WHEN FINANCIAL PROBLEMS AFFECT YOUR MARRIAGE . . .

. . . there a couple of things you
need to do.
Guys, she is scared.
She is afraid in a place you don't have.
You need to give her some more
reassuring hugs.
Gals, he is not feeling like Sir Galahad.
He's feeling pretty incompetent
so tell him you love him not because of
what he makes.
Don't let money trouble take
your marriage.

WHAT SHOULD I DO IF I WIN THE LOTTERY?

I do not like lotteries. As with all forms of gambling, the odds are always against you, whether or not you plan to use your winnings for selfish or unselfish reasoning. Listen to your odds: your odds of winning the lottery are 1 in 80,000,000; your odds of dying in a plane crash are 1 in 250,000; your odds of freezing to death are 1 in 3,000,000; your odds of being electrocuted are 1 in 350,000. The ODDS ARE AGAINST YOU. YOU WILL NOT WIN! Yet you still say, "But Dave, it's just for fun!" No, it's not for fun. Losing money is not fun!

However, in the miniscule chance that you actually win the lottery, it's a real high likelihood that you are going to lose the money unless you have the maturity and character to handle it. Just ask the woman who won $500,000 and went broke in three years.

MY HUSBAND JUST LEFT ME. HOW DO I PROTECT MY CREDIT?

If your name is on the credit cards, you are liable. So you need to remove your name from everything. Removing your name does not remove liability for past charges—you still owe on those—but it does keep you from being responsible for future charges by him.

Close the accounts today, immediately. At least take your name off of them so that you won't be liable for anything else that he spends.

Clean out the bank accounts, take out your half of the money, and get your name off the credit card accounts today. If he runs charges up, you're personally liable until you get your name off those accounts. Call the credit card companies, and then overnight a certified letter removing your name from the account.

Doing these things doesn't mean the marriage is over. You can always rejoin the accounts later if you reconcile.

If you don't reconcile, you can negotiate as part of the divorce settlement that your ex pays the bills for what he charged during the separation.

MY SPOUSE'S SPENDING IS SINKING THE FAMILY. SHOULD WE CALL IT QUITS?

I get a lot of calls from people whose marriages are in big trouble. Anyone who listens to my radio show or reads my books knows that I always urge couples to work out their problems.

I don't think it is time to call it quits. Unless you're married to some kind of addict who is destroying the family with obsessive compulsive spending, there is no need to throw in the towel.

A spender gets an emotional high when making a purchase. The skin temperature changes, palms get a little sweaty, pupils dilate, endorphins are released in the brain, and there is excitement. This can be overcome.

Stuffitis is not an incurable disease. It just takes a little maturity and growing up.

I do not tell people to file bankruptcy, and I do not tell people to file for divorce.

WE'VE SEPARATED AND NOW I MIGHT BE BANKRUPT. SHOULD I FILE?

Don't file for bankruptcy. This would be a mistake.

I want you to try to reconcile this relationship. That is always my first piece of advice.

However, if you decide to divorce, I want you to think of the following options.

- Your ex will and must be responsible for some of the debt.

- Anything that has your name on it, you need to monitor it and make sure your ex pays on it.

- You need a divorce attorney to tell you your rights.

You're probably not bankrupt. But you are scared and hurt and mad. You're also a little bit confused, but you're not bankrupt. Your income could cover some of the problems, and there are some assets that you can sell. Remember that you are not bankrupt; you just need to take care of your basic necessities and get out of debt.

MY EX ISN'T PAYING CHILD SUPPORT, AND I DON'T EARN MUCH. HOW CAN I MAKE IT?

You have four basic needs you must meet before anyone gets paid. You must have food, keep the lights on, make sure that the car is running, and pay the rent. Be sure to overfund your food allotment, because that category is always bigger than we think. Don't you dare pay anyone anything until you take care of those four basic things.

Once you have gotten that far, you can pay off some bills. You have to sit down and write a budget. You can go a long way if you are warm and have a full stomach, but you must write down where every dollar is going.

After that, you go and find this character who left you and your children and get him to start paying the child support. If he still refuses to pay up, a judge certainly will make him do it.

WE'RE TRYING TO ADOPT. SHOULD WE WAIT TO PAY CASH, OR SHOULD WE BORROW THE MONEY?

Children are blessings and parenthood is a wonderful experience. It's the best thing I've done since I've been on this planet. I really can't put myself in your shoes about adopting, but I do know that it is wise to pay cash for everything.

I do not encourage you to borrow. You may be forced to delay the adoption or go about it in a different way, and the Lord will then bless you with a child without your having to borrow money. You want children, not debt. Try to have patience and allow God to provide you with the opportunity.

There are dreamers and there are planners; the planners make their dreams come true.
EDWIN LOUIS COLE

WHY SHOULD WE TEACH KIDS ABOUT MONEY?

Some people say, "Timmy's so young—I want him to enjoy being happy and innocent. Money is a grown-up worry, not for kids."

I say, "We're raising a whole generation with 'sucker' stamped on their foreheads because we're not teaching them."

Your job as a parent is not just to keep your child happy. You're raising a future grown-up who needs to be able to deal with grown-up matters. And if you teach little Timmy how to handle money responsibly, then grown-up Timmy will be better equipped for a richer life.

Train up a child in the way he should go:
and when he is old, he will not depart from it.
PROVERBS 22:6 NIV

WHEN SHOULD I START MY KID ON AN ALLOWANCE?

As soon as your children can begin understanding cause-and-effect, they can understand work-and-money. This can work with kids even before they start school, certainly before third grade.

It is important for children to understand how finances work, or they will make the same mistakes that you have made.

I suggest instituting a commission system as opposed to an allowance. This way you can give your children money for things that they do, like chores. This will help them realize the value of money and work. This is smart.

To bring up a child in the way he should go, travel that way yourself once in a while!
JOSH BILLINGS

WHY PAY KIDS COMMISSION FOR THINGS THEY SHOULD DO ANYWAY?

Allowance spoils a child. Commission helps a child. You can give your child money in return for their help around the house. Am I suggesting that you run a sweat shop? NO. I am suggesting that you teach your kids the meaning of money and the meaning of work. These two things are attached and you need to teach them that. Then there are different teachable moments when they spend and save money that they earned rather than money that they were simply allowed.

You have to set out in advance what things you'll pay for and what things they'll pay for. Stick to your guidelines or you'll lose control of the house.

Is "clean your room" a commission thing or a family thing? You set the rule, and you'll need to stick to it.

But in general, things like "feed the dog," "mow the lawn," and "dust the living room" make good chores for earning commission, while things like "call grandma" and "do your homework" are not appropriate for commission.

Not everything can be money driven. Some things need to be done because you're a member of the family.

How do you determine how much money to give your child? We suggest $5 for 5 chores. That is just a suggestion. Use what you can reasonably afford, as long as you teach the child that the money is there because the work is done.

WHAT'S A BASIC WAY TO TEACH MY CHILDREN HOW TO HANDLE MONEY?

If you teach children the value of work, you've built character in them. And it builds confidence in them. If you don't teach your children to work I think that's child abuse.

The Financial Peace Junior kit (ages 3–12) is a great way to teach kids the value of money. The kit includes three envelopes labeled Savings, Spending, and Giving. The money that goes into these envelopes is earned through doing chores, which are charted on a commission board—if the chores are done, the kid gets money; if the chores are not done, the child doesn't get money. Simple. This teaches the children the value of earning money.

The Spending envelope lets kids still be kids and enjoy the instant pleasures of buying toys and treats.

The Savings envelope teaches children the importance of saving for future use. I tell my kids when they are very young that they must save money if they ever want to buy a car.

The Giving envelope is a way to teach children that giving is a part of life. If you're in the church parking lot and you hand your kid $2 to take to the Children's Church collection plate, that kid gets no spiritual blessing and does not understand. The child was just a courier, bringing your money to the offering. But when children bring money that they earned, then they understand that giving is a part of life.

AREN'T PRIVATE SCHOOLS AND PRIVATE LESSONS INVESTMENTS INTO A CHILD'S FUTURE?

Whether it's an investment or not, I wouldn't take out a loan to cover tuition. However, a lot of private schools have tuition plans where they accept payments throughout the year. Don't obligate yourself to money you don't have, but the payments may be doable.

When your child has a gift—whether athletic, artistic, or academic—it's tempting to pour loads of time and money into developing that gift. But you have to be reasonable about it.

What is "reasonable" is a percentage of your life. You cannot live for a 10-year-old's golf game or piano lessons.

If you are going into debt, this is not reasonable. You need to determine what part of your annual income is reasonable to spend on your child's activities. If there is a good balance, then this is fine, but your family as a whole must come first. Save for college. Save for retirement. Have an emergency fund set up. If you are doing this, then it is fine to support your child's gift.

SHOULD YOU EVER BUY A CAR FOR YOUR CHILD?

I think people who buy new BMWs for their 16-year-olds are brain-damaged.

The best thing to do for your kids is have them buy their own cars. Whatever they save is whatever they will be able to spend on their vehicles. When you buy new cars for teenagers you're setting them up for a life of ridiculous expectations. Think about their future. If you have enough cash set aside, you and your child could agree on a matching plan to help buy the car. Whatever your kid saves, you'll match. That's what Sharon and I did with our kids.

If you already have an older car that is paid for and your family is not in a financial crisis, it's fine to give a hand-me-down car to your child. If you have bills that are not paid, sell the car and pay them.

Also, if your child won't need the hand-me-down car for another few years, take into consideration how much additional depreciation will occur over that time. It might be a better deal to sell the car for a higher price now, then buy a less-expensive car when your child needs one. Or it's possible that the value won't drop much more, so you won't lose anything by just holding on to the vehicle.

MY KID WON'T SPEND HER MONEY. WHAT SHOULD I DO?

Generally, a person is either a spender or a saver. Our job as parents is to accentuate their strengths and stretch them in their weaknesses.

Most of my advice is for people who are too inclined to spend and spend and spend, so having a "saver" is a good problem.

But one of the purposes of money is to have fun, so I would encourage my saver to spend a little. You need spending in order to teach wise purchasing. No spending at all means there are no teachable moments. So force the spending occasionally.

*I have never believed that any success
outside the home can compensate for failure within it.*
DAVID GARDNER

A little bit of
controlled pain when
you're 6 will change
your life when you're 36.

I'M BROKE AND MY SON MOVED BACK IN. WHAT SHOULD I DO?

Many parents are still supporting their grown children and are wondering why they are broke.

You are in financial stress, but you still choose to support your adult son who is not showing financial responsibility. You continue to pay his bills! This is a "man" who's making bad choices, and it's time to quit supporting him! You cannot support grown children who make bad choices and be anything but broke yourself.

Your family's financial problems will persist until you realize that you are not doing your son a favor by paying for his financial mistakes. I highly recommend professional family counseling.

Go check out the book *Boundaries* by Dr. Henry Cloud. It will help you a lot.

MY PARENTS ARE FINANCIALLY IRRESPONSIBLE. HOW CAN I HELP THEM? HOW CAN I FORGIVE THEM FOR TEACHING ME THEIR BAD HABITS?

Most parents do not want their children's advice. It's just a fact of life. They do not want correction from their own children, especially if it's unsolicited. The best thing you can do to help your parents is give them your personal testimony, give them a resource like this book to start them thinking, and just keep the option open so that they can come to you if they want to.

Changing your family tree means building wealth and building character in your children so that they can manage money properly. Otherwise the wealth you leave them will be more of a curse than a blessing.

We need to reach a point, no matter how old we are, where we realize that our parents are humans and humans make mistakes. This is how it works. You need to not only realize this, but forgive them.

The deal is this: it's time to get over it. Lay it down. That's being a grown-up. Once you are able to do this, you will be breathing fresh air.

If you aim at nothing,
you will hit it every time.

ZIG ZIGLAR

A budget is telling your money
where to go instead
of wondering where it went.

JOHN C. MAXWELL

BUDGETING

THE WORD "budget" has gotten a bum rap. It basically is just a plan. When you budget you're just spending on paper, on purpose, before the month begins. The problem is that many people view a budget as a kind of straight jacket that keeps them contained. "Freedom" and "budget" just don't seem to go together.

However, when you see that a budget is just spending your money on purpose and with intention, you'll actually experience more freedom than before you budgeted. Many people report finding more money than they thought they had when they create a realistic budget and stay with it.

Here is some helpful advice about budgeting:

1. It won't be perfect the first time you do it. It will start working much better after three or four months.

2. Spend it all on paper before the month begins.

3. Overfund your groceries category. Most people underfund that category.

4. Husbands (if applicable) need to loosen up and quit using the budget as a whipping tool on their wives.

5. If married, both spouses need to do the budget together. The preacher said ". . . and you are one."

HOW DO I GET STARTED ON MANAGING MY MONEY?

To get a handle on your spending and budget ask these questions:
- How much income do I have coming in? Include everything.
- How much do I have going out in bills every month?
- Is my spouse (if you have one) working with me to get a handle on this?

You need a written game plan. John Maxwell says, "A budget is telling your money where to go, instead of wondering where it went."

You don't have to start with a perfect month. Start where you are. Write down what you have today. Income and expenses (bills). Spend all your income on paper before the month begins.

Do it all on purpose, all on paper, all with your spouse. Then you'll have a game plan.

Also, many engaged couples create practice budgets. But after you've put the practice budget together, you each should go off and pay your own bills. You don't need any joint property or joint bills until you've said your vows. Practice budgets are good for getting you accustomed to the give and take required to make a marriage thrive.

WHAT ARE SOME TIPS FOR STICKING TO A BUDGET?

Write it down. A budget is not a form of medieval torture! It is YOUR game plan, where YOU tell YOUR money what YOU want it to do. This isn't rocket science! Just give every dollar a name on paper.

Stay away from places that tempt you to spend. If you have a problem sticking to a budget, it could be that you are immature. It could be that you can't stay out of the mall! It's not smart for an alcoholic to hang out at a bar.

Try the envelope system. Take some envelopes, write the budget categories on the envelopes, and use only the allotted money to purchase specific things. If an envelope is empty, don't buy anything else in that budget category. Easy as pie.

Stay motivated! Don't give up! A budget is there to help you. It is a tool you use because you have hope that your financial situation can and will get better. One thing that can steal your hope is dwelling on the failures of the past or the fear that you will never get to the end. To avoid this, break your plan down into smaller goals. You can change your financial picture. You can change your family tree. Stay motivated!

WHAT IS THE ENVELOPE SYSTEM?

Are you on a budget and still over-spending? Are you trying to figure out the best way to organize your finances and spend wisely?

Here are simple rules for starting a cash envelope system.

Budget each paycheck. "Budget" is a dirty word to most people, but you must budget down to the last dime if you're going to successfully implement the envelope system.

Divide and conquer. Of course, there will be budget items that you cannot include in your envelope system, like bills paid by check or automatic withdrawal. However, you can create categories like food, gas, clothing, and entertainment.

Fill'er Up. After you've categorized your cash expenses, fill each envelope with the money allotted for it in your budget. For example, if you allow $100 for clothing, put $100 in cash in your clothing envelope for the month.

When it's gone, it's gone. Once you've spent all the money in a given envelope, you're done spending for that category. If you go on a shopping spree and spend the $100 in your clothing envelope, you can't spend any more on clothes until you budget for that category again. That means no visits to the ATM to withdraw more money!

Don't be tempted. While debit cards can't get you directly into debt, if used carelessly they can cause you to over-spend. There's something psychological about spending cash that hurts more than swiping a piece of plastic. If spending cash whenever possible can become a habit, you'll be less likely to over-spend or buy on impulse.

Give it time. It will take a few months to perfect your envelope system. Don't give up after a month or two if it's not clicking. You'll get the hang of it and see how beneficial the envelope system is as you dump debt, build wealth and achieve financial peace!

See . . . simple!

Certainly, some bills may come in at different times of the month, so you'll need to adjust your written gameplan to take it one step further. You need to make the budget based upon your pay periods. Say that you get paid twice per month. If you can write down which bills you plan on paying from each paycheck, you will not be left with a surprise bill. Spend each month's income on paper before it comes in, and that means spending each individual paycheck on paper as well.

I also have no problem with you adding an envelope with money just to "blow." As long as you and your spouse have agreed on it, you are fine. There should be no lying. Agree on your budget, agree on your blow money, and be open. Blow money can be anything you want it to be. There are no rules on that envelope, unlike money in the "entertainment" envelope that is used specifically for entertainment.

MONEYMATTERS

MY INCOME IS IRREGULAR. HOW CAN I MAKE A BUDGET?

It is difficult to budget when your income is not predictable. You must determine your lowest possible income and make your budget based on those numbers. Then make a list of all the things that you were unable to do based on your lowest income. Prioritize that list. What is the one thing you would do first if the money became available? Number the list accordingly. Then, follow it. The original budget is always your priority, and any extra money can be used to cover the second list.

Well done is better than well said.
BENJAMIN FRANKLIN

MONEY ACTION

A VERY BASIC BUDGET

ITEM	SUBTOTAL	TOTAL	ACTUALLY SPENT	% OF INCOME (RECOMMENDED)
CHARITABLE GIFTS		_____	_____	(10%-15%) _____
SAVING				
Emergency Fund	_____		_____	
Retirement	_____	_____	_____	(5%-10%) _____
HOUSING				
Rent/Mortgage	_____		_____	
Insurance	_____		_____	
Fees & Taxes	_____	_____	_____	(25%-30%) _____
UTILITIES				
Electricity	_____		_____	
Water	_____		_____	
Gas	_____		_____	
Phone	_____		_____	
Trash	_____		_____	
Cable	_____	_____	_____	(5%-10%) _____
***FOOD**				
*Grocery	_____		_____	
*Restaurants	_____	_____	_____	(10%-15%) _____
TRANSPORTATION				
Car Payment(s)	_____		_____	
*Gas & Oil	_____		_____	
*Repairs & Tires	_____		_____	
Insurance	_____		_____	
Replacement	_____	_____	_____	(10%-15%) _____
MEDICAL/HEALTH				
Insurance	_____			
Doctor/Dentist Bills	_____		_____	
Medicine	_____	_____	_____	(5%-10%) _____
PERSONAL *Clothing				
Life Insurance	_____			
Child Care	_____		_____	
*Grooming	_____		_____	
Education	_____		_____	
Gifts	_____		_____	
Child Support	_____		_____	
Miscellaneous	_____		_____	
*Blow	_____		_____	
RECREATION				(5%-10%) _____
*Entertainment	_____			
Vacation	_____		_____	
DEBTS (hopefully $0)	_____			(5%-10%) _____
Credit Card(s)				
Student Loan(s)	_____		_____	
Other(s)	_____		_____	
	_____	_____		(5%-10%) _____
TOTALS				

* Use the Envelope System   _____

It is absolutely okay for a Christian to want to be a millionaire, because as Christians we know that no matter how much we have, we own nothing. We are simply managers of the resources God has given us. If we can manage God's money, whether $100 or $1 million, we are okay.

Money that comes easily disappears quickly, but money that is gathered little by little will grow.

PROVERBS 13:11 NCV

SAVING & INVESTING

SAVING is necessary because its ability to stabilize your finances is remarkable. Without saving, you aren't really prepared for the future.

Savings should be boring. It is best kept in CDs or money market accounts, savings accounts, or even plain old cookie jars. That's because the money you put into savings isn't meant to stay there long term. It is the money you plan to use for something within the next five years. Money you plan to use in the near future doesn't need to be subjected to risk; it needs to be safe, so that it is still there when you want it, regardless of how the stock markets are performing that day. For instance, if you're saving for a car, I would use a money market account with a mutual fund company. Do not put money into a mutual fund unless you are to leave it alone for at least five years.

Investing is a subject that can generate very diverse reactions from many people. Some people get excited and the juices start flowing when the topic is introduced. Others start to get nervous, break out in sweat and are easily are extreme. Somewhere in the middle is where you'll find me.

My first principle when it comes to investing is not to mess with investing until you've completed your first three baby steps. Once you've done that, then you are ready to invest. You are ready to fully fund 15 percent into pre-tax retirement plans and Roth IRA, if eligible.

The second major principle I teach is this: never invest in anything you don't understand. Don't invest in something because your brother-in-law says, "You gotta do this!" This includes online trading—a mutual fund that spends $54 million in research understands a whole lot more about stocks than you do.

IS SAVING REALLY THAT IMPORTANT?

Do you know what it is going to feel like when you wake up at 65 and broke? You have to plan. You have to save money. You have to save for emergencies, you have to save for the future, you have to save to buy items and replace cars. If you don't save, you will always live in debt. You will always be stressed about money. You will always be broke.

Turn off the TV and think. RIGHT NOW! How are you going to buy your next car? How are you going to retire? How will you survive if you are laid off?

As long as you have payments, as long as you have stuffitis, as long as you entertain yourself at the mall you will be B–R–O–K–E. You can afford to save if you stop buying everything.

You have to draw a line in sand and cry out "That's it! I don't want to live like everyone else. Normal is broke, and I want to be WEIRD!"

WHAT IS THE SECRET TO SAVING?

Saving money is not a matter of math. You will not save money when you get that next raise, you will not save money when that car is paid off, you will not save money when the kids are grown. You will only save money when it becomes an emotional priority.

We all know we need to save, but most people don't save like they know they need to. Why? Because they have competing goals. The goal to save isn't a high enough priority to delay that purchase of the pizza, or the DVD player, or the new computer, or the china cabinet. So we purchase, buy, consume all our dollars away or, worse yet, go into debt to buy these things. That debt means monthly payments that control our paychecks and make us say things like, "we just don't make enough to save any money." Wrong, wrong, wrong!!! We DO make enough to save money; we just aren't willing to quit spoiling ourselves with our little projects or pleasures to have enough left to save. I don't care what you make, you can save money. It just has to become a big enough priority to you.

If a doctor told you that your child was dying and could only be saved with a $15,000 operation that your insurance would not cover and could only be performed nine months from today, could you save $15,000? The answer is yes! Of course you could! You would sell things, you would stop any spending that wasn't required to survive, and you would take two extra jobs. For that short nine months, you would become a saving madman (or madwoman). You would give up virtually anything to accomplish that $15,000 goal. SAVING WOULD BECOME A PRIORITY.

The secret to saving? FOCUSED EMOTION. The secret to saving money is to make it a priority and that is done ONLY when you get some healthy anger or fear and then focus that emotion on your personal decisions. Harnessing that emotion will make you move yourself to the top of your creditor list. Then ask yourself, "which bill is the most important. After tithing, who should I pay first this month?" The answer is, YOU! Until you pay God first, then you, then everyone and everything else, you will never save money.

The advertisers and marketing community are affecting our emotions every day and taking every dollar we have by making us see our WANTS as NEEDS. It is time for this to stop. Emotions make great slaves, but they are lousy masters. No matter how educated or sophisticated we are, if we are not saving all we should be, we are being ruled by emotions, not harnessing them as financial planning slaves.

In the house of the wise are stores of choice food and oil, but a foolish man devours all he has.
PROVERBS 21:20

HOW DO I GET STARTED WITH INVESTING?

With a lot of mutual funds you can get in for a $250 or $500 lump sum. This initial amount can be as low as $25 if you decide to give to the fund monthly.

If you are going to put in less than $10,000, I would suggest a calm growth and income fund that has been open for longer than five years.

If you are going to put in more than $10,000, remember to spread out your investments. I suggest the following distribution: 25 percent growth, 25 percent growth and income, 25 percent aggressive growth, and 25 percent international.

If you want to invest in real estate, start slowly. Real estate is a good plan only with money lying around so you don't get into trouble. The real estate investors I know who are still around after more than twenty years did it with mostly cash. Investing with cash takes longer, but you don't wind up broke and bankrupt. Study and read while you pile up cash, and then buy your first property at a serious bargain.

WHAT ARE THE BASICS OF INVESTING?

The difference between saving and investing is that savings accounts are for money that you will want to use within the next five years. If you are willing to leave money alone for more than five years, then you can begin investing.

When most people think about investing they think about buying stocks. Buying single stocks is dangerous. When you put all your money in one company, you are risking everything. This is unwise. Bonds are just about as risky as stock. What is a bond? It's a debt that a company has and you are the one loaning the company money. If the company goes broke, you will likely not be paid.

I recommend mutual funds. This is where many people mutually invest in a fund, which represents several companies. It's much lower risk. Another great place to put money is in real estate—IF you can do it without going into debt.

An annuity is a savings account with an insurance company. One type is a fixed annuity, basically a bad, bad investment. The other type is a variable annuity, which has a mutual fund inside it. Don't do this within a retirement fund, because you'll be paying double fees.

So, what should you NEVER EVER EVER DO??? NEVER do day trading. NEVER invest in something unless you understand how it works.

WILL I RETIRE WITH MORE MONEY IF IT'S INVESTED IN A ROTH OR A TRADITIONAL IRA?

You'll have more money with a Roth.

Because the Roth IRA growth is tax free, you get to keep all the money in your Roth IRA.

You have to pay taxes on the growth in a traditional IRA, so if you were to put the same amount of money into a traditional and into a Roth IRA, in the end the you would be able to keep all the money you draw out of the Roth IRA.

For example, if you have $1,000 dollars to invest, when you bring it home you only have $700 (assuming a 30 percent tax bracket). If you put the $1,000 in a 401(k) (pre–tax) and $700 in your Roth (after tax) and they both grow the same amount, that $300 extra dollars grows into exactly enough to pay the taxes on the growth. So it is a wash (Roth grows tax free).

But what if you save like a maniac? Your mandatory withdrawals at the age of 70 will put you in the top tax bracket. So my plan will assuredly win there because you'll be taxed higher on that extra $300.

If you put $1,000 in each then there is barely any comparison. You have to pay taxes on the growth in the 401(k) and no taxes on the growth of the Roth. This is life here, not theory.

WHAT TYPES OF INVESTMENT PLANS MIGHT I BE OFFERED?

• *401(k) Plan:* A corporate pre-tax contributory plan, payroll deducted, tax-deferred, with a selection of investment options to invest in. Most plans also include company matching* with a vesting schedule based on years of employment.

• *403(b) Plan:* A non-profit pre-tax contributory plan (clergy, some medical personnel, school teachers, etc.), payroll deducted, growing tax-deferred, with a selection of investment options to invest in. Some plans provide company matching.*

• *457 Plan:* A deferred compensation pre-tax contributory plan, payroll deducted, growing tax-deferred, with a selection of options to invest in. Most plans provide minimal matching.*

• *Thrift Savings Plan:* A government agency pre-tax contributory plan, payroll deducted, growing tax-deferred, with a selection of five managed investment options to invest in. A minimal agency match* is available. We recommend 40 percent in the "C" fund, 40 percent in the "S" fund, and 20 percent in the "I" fund.

• *Simple IRA/401(k):* A smaller company pre-tax contributory plan, payroll deducted, growing tax-deferred, with a selection of investment options to invest in. Normally, there is a mandatory match*, with much lower administrative costs.

• *Simplified Employee Pension Plan (SEPP):* A self-employed person may contribute pre-tax up to 15 percent of their net business profit, growing tax-deferred, with a self-directed selection of investment options to invest in.

I usually recommend you invest up to the match, then pour into your Roth.

HOW DO I SET SHORT-TERM AND LONG-TERM INVESTING GOALS?

Most people have the best intentions, yet often fail to write down specific goals they desire to reach financially. Your goal is to determine in clear simple terms what your short-term and long-term goals are by asking questions. You help yourself by asking questions of your spouse to draw out your priorities. One way to do this is by making a list of what is important to each of you, listing from most important to least important. Compare your lists so that both of you have your priorities included. Then integrate them and begin formulating a plan to get there.

Short-term goals can be something you want to save for or purchase within the next month, this calendar year, or the next two to three years. It is helpful to explore a simple tool called a "Needs and Wants" list. Brainstorm what you need versus what you want. List them. After brainstorming, ask yourself three simple questions about each listed item.

1. "If we didn't purchase this item this year would it make a big difference to both of us?" If it doesn't, it slides over to the Wants list.

2. On the Needs list, ask, "If we could only purchase one of these items by saving for it this year, which one would we prioritize first?" Then, choose which would be the second and so on for both the Needs list and the Wants list.

3. "How much will each item cost?" Begin researching to see what these particular items cost.

When you have finished answering these questions, total the dollar amount of the Needs list and divide by twelve months. When the dollar amount is known, place it in your budget as a non–monthly annual savings goal and begin saving for it. Cash will stretch further and you will find yourselves dealing for the items in cash and getting a better price.

Long–term goals are usually those that you plan on completing beyond three years from now. Formulate questions that help you determine what specific goals you have based on where you are in life. Some of these questions can address:

· Debt elimination
· Retirement
· College funding for children
· Wedding funding for children
· Automobile replacement
· Special travel plans
· Paying off present home
· Saving for large ticket items
· Vacation home
· Major remodeling on home
· Financial freedom
· Developing your own business
· Charitable giving goals

IS A SMALL MUTUAL FUND A GOOD WEDDING GIFT?

Instead of another set of guest towels or crystal for the dining room, you're giving the happy couple a piece of paper saying they have a new $500 investment in a mutual fund. Wow!

Let's assume 12 percent annual growth and that they hold the investment for thirty years without adding anything to it. That $500 would grow to about $18,000. If they kept it for fifty years, it would be worth $200,000. That's one heck of a wedding present! And those pretty towels won't be nearly that nice in fifty years.

I have never seen a monument erected to a pessimist.
PAUL HARVEY

I HAD A 401(K) WITH A COMPANY THAT WENT BROKE. DO I STILL GET THE MONEY?

Yes! You can check your old pay stubs and find out who the administrator is for your 401(k). Just give them a call.

My suggestion is to roll it over into an IRA. If that does not work, you can contact your state or the Securities Exchange Commission.

A 401(k) is not an asset of a company, so if the company goes broke, your money is still sitting there.

However, you cannot roll a 401(k) from a company until you work there no longer. If your 401(k) is all in single stocks GET OUT! Put it in good growth mutual funds.

And in case you're worried about your mutual fund broker going out of business, relax. There is no risk in having just one mutual fund broker. The only thing a broker does is line you up with a mutual fund company. If the broker were to go out of business, your funds would still be there.

SHOULD I CASH OUT OR ROLL OVER MY 401(K)?

Do not cash out your 401(k) until you are ready to retire; one in five U.S. workers are making this mistake and now have loans against their 401(k) funds. Withdrawing money from your 401(k) plan can result in major taxes and penalties. In some cases, people who withdraw early end up with half as much as they had originally.

For example, an American worker in their 30s has about $33,000 in their 401(k). If they leave it alone until they're 65, it will be worth $578,000. If they cash it out now, after taxes and penalties, it will only be worth about $18,000. Unfortunately, more than half of the people in their 30s, who are laid off, cash out their 401(k) plans.

If you are changing employers, roll your 401(k) into an IRA. Of course you're busy when you're making such a big change in our life, but rolling over the $4,713.16 in your 401(k) must be a priority.

It is not smart to cash out your 401(k) and pay 40 percent in penalties and taxes. If you're smart you'll just roll it into an IRA and not touch it until you retire.

Fill out the rollover form. Thirty minutes of your time could be worth over $100,000 by the time you retire.

HOW CAN I INVEST IN MUTUAL FUNDS WITH COMPANIES THAT ALIGN WITH MY SPIRITUAL VALUES?

The first thing to be sensitive to is God's guidance. If through your prayer time you feel uneasy about investing in a certain fund, you should not do it.

There are services available online that rate funds and the companies that they represent. This can help you somewhat by letting you know the "rating" of a company with regard to their morals or cleanliness.

Remember this: if you own stock in a company, the company itself does not get any money from you. You are owning part of the company, not funding their business. Be aware of this difference. You may feel unethical about owning a portion of the company, but you are still in no way funding their growth.

You might want to check out the Timothy Plan® (TimothyPlan.com), which avoids investing in companies that are involved in practices contrary to Judeo–Christian principles, or visit SocialInvest.org, a national nonprofit membership organization promoting the concept, practice, and growth of socially responsible investing.

When I was a child, I spoke like a child, I understood as a child, I thought as a child: but when I became a man, I put away childish things.

1 CORINTHIANS 13:11 NIV

Character cannot be developed in ease and quiet. Only through experience of trial and suffering can the soul be strengthened, vision cleared, ambition inspired, and success achieved.

HELEN KELLER

20-SOMETHINGS, COLLEGE & STUDENT LOANS

YOU could be a millionaire (multiple times over) by age 55 or so if you pay attention to the information in this chapter. How can I possibly make this claim? Simple. If you make smart choices now—and avoid stupid ones—you'll reap the benefit of making wise financial decisions over a 30–year period.

Major changes normally occur in the twenties: graduating from college, starting a career, finding your mate, and even starting a family. Wow! Behind these changes are choices that shape us for the rest of our lives. Things like:

- Do I get student loans to pay for college? (NO!)
- When do I buy my first home?
- How should newlyweds handle their finances?
- When should I start investing for the long term?
- What are the four NEVERS of college saving ?

If you want to be normal, or like the typical college graduate—flat broke—then just do what normal people do. But if you want to make wise financial decisions and be able to live the next 40+ years with financial peace-of-mind, then dig into this chapter.

This is a great season of life. Your college years will be some of the most memorable ones you'll have. However, if you want to make sure they are pleasant memories, then you need to avoid loans and credit cards. The average college graduate in 2002 graduated with over $27,500 in student loans. Add another $6,000 in credit card debt and the typical graduate walks across the platform with $30,000 in debt before getting that first job! That's a terrible way to begin a career or build a life.

If you're a parent and you still have some time before Junior is in college, then you want to make sure you take advantage of other investment tools to help pay for college, especially ESAs. Don't know what those are? Then read on.

WHAT ARE THE FOUR NEVERS OF COLLEGE SAVING?

1. Never save for college using insurance.
2. Never save for college using savings bonds. (Only 5%–6% growth)
3. Never save for college using zero-coupon bonds.
(Only 6%–8% growth)
4. Never save for college using pre-paid college tuition.
(Only 7% inflation rate)

A generation ago there were a thousand men to every opportunity...
while today there are a thousand opportunities to every man.
HENRY FORD

HOW CAN I AVOID STUDENT LOANS?

Start with grants and scholarships, which means it would be a great idea if your GPA was much higher than average. Good grades are an investment. Students in the top ten percent of their classes have many more options.

• Work part–time if you need the money. I'm sure that went over like a lead balloon, but you need income.

• Attend an affordable local college to get your first few years of required classes over with, then transfer to the school of your dreams IF you can pay cash.

Patience is better than strength.
Controlling your temper is better than capturing a city.
PROVERBS 16:32 NCV

WHEN DOES IT MAKE SENSE TO GO TO COLLEGE?

Going to college is not necessary to exist on this planet. Education is absolutely wonderful and vital, and I think everyone who wants to go to college should. Just don't go thinking that a diploma will be your ticket to a successful life.

Don't get me wrong. I think education is extremely important. However, going into major debt in order to get a degree that you will never use is ridiculous. When I hire people for my company, I don't look only at the degrees they have. I look at desire, attitude, diligence, people skills, and other qualities. These are the things that will determine if they are successful, not necessarily a degree.

I think there are two reasons to pursue an education.

1) If a degree in your chosen field will open doors to career opportunities. The truth is that in many fields a degree will not open doors. Consider whether all the costs balance against the financial rewards.

2) To improve your life quality through the pursuit of knowledge. If your reason is personal growth and to do what God has called you to, make sure you go slow and pay cash to avoid getting into trouble. Use wisdom for the sake of your family. Don't make your future hostage to student loans.

WHAT ARE THE BASICS ON ESAS, EDUCATIONAL IRAS, 529S, AND UTMAS?

The Education IRA is the same thing as an ESA (Educational Savings Account). The ESA is basically buying a mutual fund and stamping it "ESA." You must make less than $200,000 annually, married filing jointly. You can contribute up to $2,000 annually per child. You can have several ESAs, but the total of them can only be $2,000 annually per child. That money will grow completely tax-free when used for higher education. You can move them around to different mutual funds as well.

Like ESAs, 529 plans all grow tax free, but you have significantly less control than with an ESA.

There are three kinds of 529 plans.

The first is pre-paid college tuition. Never do this. The rate of return is based on the inflation rate, which is currently around 7 percent. This is a terrible rate of return for a long-term investment.

The other types of 529s allow you to invest up to $10,000 annually. With the Life-Phase 529, you give the money to a 529 administrating company, and they invest it based upon your child's age. You have no control over where they invest. They will be very conservative, and will usually yield an 8 percent to 9 percent rate of return. The Static-Plan 529 tells you which mutual funds the money is going into. You can't choose the funds, but you see where it is going. You are still locked in, so I don't like these. There are some 529s that are now allowing you to see and choose the mutual funds and even move them if needed. This type is fine AFTER you fund ESAs.

A UTMA, Uniform Transfer to Minors Act, (also known as an UGMA) means you are opening the mutual fund in the child's name. You are merely the custodian of the money. At age 21, this money belongs to the child and is in their control. As you go along, teach them what this means, so they are not surprised with $125,000 (could happen!) at age 21. Who knows where they'll spend it!?

The UTMA will basically grow tax-free, the reason being that the first $750 that it earns per year is tax free. If the child is under 14 years old, the next $750 (beyond the first $750) is taxed at the child's rate, and anything beyond that is taxed at the parents' rate. Once they turn 14, everything beyond the first $750 is taxed at the child's rate.

I recommend the ESA. You have the control. Unless your child is going to Harvard, if you start while they're young, $2,000 a year is going to put them anywhere you want them to go. It won't be enough to put them through medical school, but it grows tax free, you retain control, and there is a great rate of return. If you make over $200,000 or would like to invest more than $2,000 annually, then the flexible-529 is the next best option.

MY SON LOST HIS SCHOLARSHIP. WHAT SHOULD WE DO?

You should help your son with his education only if you can afford it. If putting your son through college is going to jeopardize the welfare of the rest of the family, then it is unwise.

Education is important, but it is not the only way to survive in this culture. If it is impossible to pay for schooling, he can still make it in life.

With regard to him losing the scholarship, perhaps he can beg his professors for extra work to bring up his grades. Also, he should apply for scholarships all summer. There are plenty of $1,000 scholarships out there, and those add up.

The bottom line is that you, the parents, shouldn't feel guilty because you "failed" your son. You didn't. Your son, an adult, failed and lost his scholarship. Now you are placed in the position to pay for something you cannot afford. I want to free you from this guilt. Whatever you can do is good enough.

I'M A STUDENT AND I'M BEHIND ON BILLS. WHAT SHOULD I DO?

So many college students have debts beyond their eyeballs. Big car payment. Credit card debt. They don't know what to do.

You think it's okay to just go to school full-time and not pay your bills? I don't! You need to pay off your credit card debt and sell your car retail to minimize the damage, as opposed to selling it back to the dealer and just getting trade-in value.

You might have to take a semester, at least, off from school and go get your mess cleaned up by working three jobs. Then you can go back to school without all this pressure and actually think about what you're doing!

More 20-somethings think they will see a UFO sooner than they will receive Social Security. They are right! Social Security is pretty insecure. Stop depending on the promise of Social Security and start taking care of yourself!

Money is like manure.
If you leave it in a pile, it stinks.
But if you spread it around,
it does a lot of good.

God has given us two hands—
one to receive with and the other to give
with. We are not cisterns made
for hoarding; we are channels made
for sharing.

REV. BILLY GRAHAM

STEWARDSHIP

"**WE** make a living by what we get, but we make a life by what we give."

Save, Spend, and Give—my big three principles. Most people forget about the giving part because they think I only scream, "Save, save, save!!"

Giving liberates the soul of the giver. You never walk away feeling badly. Whether through a tithe, charitable contribution, or gift to a friend in need—give away at least some of your money. Not only does it generate good feelings, it generates contentment.

Remember, no one has ever become poor by giving.

If you cannot be trusted with things that belong to someone else, who will give you things of your own?
LUKE 16:12 NCV

IS IT ACCEPTABLE TO 'PAUSE' TITHING IN TOUGH FINANCIAL TIMES?

The Bible does not mention anything about "pausing" tithing, and neither does it say that we will go to hell if we do not tithe. The tithe, which is a scriptural mandate, was not instituted for God's benefit because He already has all the money He needs. He does not need our money.

So why does He ask us to give 10 percent to Him? Tithing was created for our benefit. It is to teach us how to keep God first in our lives and how to be unselfish people. Unselfish people make better husbands, wives, friends, relatives, employees, and employers. God is trying to teach us how to prosper over time.

Many people have observed that after they stopped tithing, their finances seemed to get worse. In the Book of Malachi, God promises that if you do not rob Him of your tithing, He will rebuke your devourers and protect you.

If you cannot live off 90 percent then you cannot live off 100 percent. It does not require a "miracle" for you to get through the month. I think that if you sit down and look at your budget, you will see that you can make it while giving 10 percent. Read the Bible and take from it what you will, and if you tithe, do it out of love for God, not guilt.

I do not beat people up for not tithing, because Jesus certainly did not, but let me encourage you to keep tithing.

IS IT RIGHT TO COUNT MY CHURCH TITHES ON MY TAX RETURNS?

You gave the money to the church. You were biblically obedient in that. The Bible also tells us to be good managers of our money. It does not diminish the sanctity of your gift to take the tax deduction. It is a way to manage the rest of the money. Take the deduction.

And later, when you get your income tax refund, remember that this is money that you've already tithed, although you're certainly welcome to devote some or all of it back to the Lord as additional thanks for His blessings.

Do not conform any longer to the pattern of this world, but be transformed by the renewing of your mind. Then you will be able to test and approve what God's will is— his good pleasing and perfect will.
ROMANS 12:2 NIV

SHOULD MY CHURCH BORROW FOR A NEW BUILDING?

Churches often are run by businessmen. They try to run the church like it's a business, and they get very offended when anyone tries to run it by the Bible.

As for the church borrowing money, I personally think this is wrong. No passage in the Bible says that good things come from borrowing, but there are many, many negative things in there referring to debt. There is not one time in the Bible God used debt as a tool to help His people.

But you can't convince anyone against his or her own will to agree with a debt-free plan.

Along a related path, sometimes a church will ask members to co-sign on the loan for a building. There is no way under the sun I would sign something like that. You will be in a deal with every single other member of the congregation. This is a recipe for disaster, a horrible deal. Nowhere in the Bible does it say that the congregation should get together to sign a note for a church building. That would be going about the Lord's work by the way of the world. Don't sign.

I'M MAKING MORE MONEY NOW. HOW SHOULD I INCREASE MY GIVING ABOVE THE TITHE?

When things are going well, it's very easy to accidentally spend all the extra income, so I would recommend that you budget what to do with it.

For example, Sharon and I set up a budget based on my salary. This budget includes giving, spending, and saving—just as I advise others to do. Then, everything else we make is divided among extra giving, extra investing, and some blow money.

The person who risks nothing, does nothing, has nothing and is nothing. They may avoid suffering and sorrow, but they cannot learn, feel, change, grow, love, and live. Chained by their certitudes, they are a slave, they have forfeited their freedom. Only a person who risks is free.

UNKNOWN

No matter who you are,
you face obstacles daily.
The people who win are the people
who refuse to let that stop them.
Work. Try. Don't give up.

Pray for good harvest . . . BUT keep
on hoeing!

SIGN ALONG A RURAL ROAD

INSURANCE

INSURANCE is very important to your financial health.

Let's talk life insurance. I solely recommend term life, not whole life, and that you get 8–10 times your salary in a good term life policy.

How about health insurance? Medical bills are one of the reasons listed most often when filing for bankruptcy. With extremely high medical costs, insurance is very important to have. It can be the difference between being prosperous and being a pauper.

While health insurance is by no means cheap, it can be affordable.

It is an absolute must to have an major medical plan that covers mainly hospital stays and big events. If you and your family are healthy, you should investigate HSAs.

An HSA (health savings account) is an insurance plan with a tax–free savings account that allows you save up for your deductible. The premium is significantly lower than traditional insurance, and the deductible is much higher. If you want co-pay and prescription benefits, you won't find them here, but if you want to save money, don't need to go the doctor every week, and qualify, an HSA is the best decision you can make.

If you go with health insurance, remember one very important rule: Low premiums equal high deductibles. This is the way to go. That high deductible might seem kind of scary, but isn't that what your emergency fund is for? With a fully funded emergency fund you can afford a higher deductible, even if it is all paid in one visit to the doctor.

There is no need to purchase specialty insurances like cancer insurance. Cancer is a scary thing, but if you get it, it will be covered by the insurance you already have. Why don't you get heart attack insurance? Same reason. Don't fork over the extra money because it is a waste.

Worry is a misuse of the imagination.
DAN ZADRA

WHAT KINDS OF INSURANCE DO I ACTUALLY NEED?

MONEY ACTION

CHECK THE ONES YOU HAVE

- Health insurance—everyone
- Auto insurance—required by law in many states
- Life insurance—I would buy term insurance (10 times your income if you have a child). The savings portion of a whole life policy is a total rip off. The interest paid on it amounts to only about 2 percent to 3 percent.
- Disability insurance—A lot of people overlook disability insurance. The saddest cases we get here in counseling are those who have no income but ongoing expenses because they became disabled. Everyone knows you need life insurance, but not everyone realizes that you need long-term disability insurance.
- Long-term care insurance—when you're over 60
- Homeowners or renters insurance

WHAT KIND OF LIFE INSURANCE SHOULD I GET FOR MY CHILD AND FOR MY SPOUSE?

I recommend a Roth IRA and life insurance for you and your spouse. Carry about ten times what each of you makes (or at least $400,000 on a stay–at–home parent).

Don't buy life insurance for your child; it is a rip off. Just get a $10,000 to $15,000 rider on your own policy to cover burial expenses in that unfortunate scenario.

Because you also are going to want to save for college in a good mutual fund using an ESA, see Chapter 6 on 20–Somethings, College & Student Loans.

Vision without action is a daydream. Action without vision is a nightmare.
JAPANESE PROVERB

WHAT SHOULD I LOOK FOR IN GOOD HOME INSURANCE?

Many insurance companies are doing away with replacement cost insurance. Replacement cost insurance replaces your home no matter what, even if you don't update your policy as the value of your home changes. Some companies have gone to policies that will only pay 120 percent of policy value, so you must continually update them. As long as your property doesn't increase in value more than 20 percent you're okay. If it goes up more, though, you're in trouble.

I would call an independent insurance agent and have him or her shop around and get you quotes.

If at first you don't succeed... try hard work.
WILLIAM FEATHER

The average person playing the lottery spends $32 a month. That same $32 a month represents over $1 million dollars in retirement if invested over a working lifetime.

It isn't what you have in your pocket that makes you thankful, but what you have in your heart.

Unknown

RETIREMENT & ESTATE PLANNING

EVERYONE knows they need to save for retirement. Not everyone does, and too many of those who do save, don't save enough. Not saving enough money for your retirement is a sure way to keep Alpo in business.

At a minimum you need to save 15 percent of your income in good growth stock mutual funds. Of course, retirement savings comes after you are out of debt and have a fully funded emergency fund. With no debts and a full emergency fund, it's much easier to save the money you need for your retirement.

Once you are ready to start funding your retirement nest egg, you will need to choose how. There are a number of different vehicles, Traditional IRAs, Roth IRAs, 401(k)s, and 403(b)s are the most common. All those letters and numbers are nothing but a cover to protect your investments from tax in one way or another. They limit the amount of money you can deposit each year, limit the amount of money you're allowed to make in order to use them, and place limits on when you can take money out.

And while you're thinking about retirement, you also need to look a little farther ahead. Estate planning isn't just for wealthy or rich people who have lots of land and money to pass on to their heirs. If you plan on dying (or even if you don't) you need a plan for how to pass on your stuff. Wow. How's that for simplicity in explaining estate planning?

We all gather stuff along life's journey. Some more than others. Some way too much, really. Whether you have a little or a lot, if you want to make sure that your niece gets that old Victrola, then you'd better write it down. And then there's your mother's tea set, and . . . see what I mean.

The best way to get rich quick is to get rich slow. When it comes to wealth building, perserverence wins. Sprinters do not. True wealth–building is hard and it takes time. If wealth–building were easy, everyone would be rich! It is tough, but once you get there, it puts you in a position to bless others and to change your family tree. It's worth it to persevere.

WHEN IS IT TOO LATE TO START SAVING FOR RETIREMENT?

It's never too late. If you waited to start saving, you'll just have to be that much more intense about saving and investing.

For instance, if you're 60 years old and have no debt, then I would save like a crazy person putting the money in growth stock mutual funds. Make sure you've saved three to six months of expenses in an emergency fund. You still can do a pretty decent job of catching up, but you're going to have to work longer than five years before retiring.

If you both are 40 years old now and you fully fund a Roth IRA at $6,000 ($3,000 for wife, $3,000 for husband) every year, you will have about $1 million tax-free when you retire at 65. But, hey, if you think you are too old to start, then maybe you could come up with that $1 million some other way. Yeah right! Get Roth IRAs! Fund them and retire securely.

IS A SEPP A GOOD PLAN FOR THE SELF-EMPLOYED?

Yes. SEPPs (Simplified Employee Pension Plans) are excellent for small companies where you are self-employed. You can save up to 15 percent of income up to a cap each year. The money you save is tax deductible.

If you make less than $150,000 annually (married filing jointly), I also strongly recommend that you max out your Roth IRA first because that growth is tax-free. But then definitely use the SEPP if you have the option.

Success is peace of mind, which is a direct result of knowing you did your best to become the best that you are capable of becoming.
JOHN WOODEN

WHAT ARE THE BEST WAYS TO SAVE FOR RETIREMENT?

This really isn't rocket science.

The Roth IRA grows completely tax-free. If you save up $4 million in a Roth IRA it is all yours. If you save that same amount in a 401(k) you will have to pay out about $1 million in taxes. That's a big difference.

Given this comparison, always take a Roth IRA when you are investing over a long period of time. You can invest $3,000 per year per individual and $6,000 per married couple. The one exception to this is if your 401(k) or 403(b) matches. This is a great deal.

So, if your company matches your 401(k), take that first. Above and beyond that, do a Roth IRA. Remember, if you save 15 percent of your income for your retirement, you will retire with dignity.

For more information about Saving and Investing, take a look at the questions starting on page 91.

SHOULD I PRE-PAY FOR MY FUNERAL?

Prepaid funerals are not a good idea. Never pre-pay a funeral. Stay away.

Case in point: Let's say that at age 40 you put $3,000 into pre-paying your funeral. The odds are that you will live to 90. (Yes, the average age of death is 74 for males and 78 for females, but if you've already lived until 40, your odds are much better.) If, instead of pre-paying your funeral, you took that same $3,000 and invested it for that same amount of time into a decent growth stock mutual fund, you would have $1,174,000 when you die! Who are you? King Tut? Come on! The truth is that funeral costs do not go up nearly as fast as a good quality investment.

It is definitely smart to pre-*arrange* your funeral—by clearly spelling out what you want—but pre-payment of your funeral is not wise.

Life is either a daring adventure, or nothing.
HELEN KELLER

WHAT IS A WILL?

A will (the formal title is usually "Last Will and Testament") is simply a document by which a person designates who will receive his or her property after his or her death.

In addition to property distribution instructions, a will can include instructions for appointment of an executor to handle the estate, appointment of a guardian for any minor children (although in most states, the court can override your appointment if deemed to be in the better interest of the children), and other directives regarding responsibilities once held by the deceased.

The person making a will is usually called the "testator", and the person receiving the property is the "heir" or "beneficiary." In most states, personal property conveyed via a will is referred to as a "bequest", while real estate is conveyed by a "devise."

This definition is derived from Tennessee state law, but it probably is similar to the definition used in your state. For more legal information about estate planning, probate, wills and living trusts please visit CityLegalGuide.com.

DO I REALLY NEED A WILL?

A recent survey found that 74 percent of Americans with children do not have a will. 39.5 percent of people say they do not have a will because of a lack of time. 26.2 percent of Americans say they do not have a will because of the cost.

That is stupid. Get a will. You need a will even if you don't have any assets. You need one especially if you have kids and you don't want the state to decide who will raise them if you die. One of the ways I prove that I love my family is by having a current will that lays out step by step what to do should anything happen to me.

To get a will, you and your spouse need to find an estate attorney. I suggest a mirror image will. That way, if one of you dies, the surviving spouse will get everything—hence the term "mirror image."

Some people try to avoid the expense of an attorney and do their wills themselves. I think this is very unwise. You can get a mirror-image will for you and your spouse for about $300. It is well worth the money to make sure that your will is done correctly.

Also, after someone has died, 98 percent of the time I would recommend that the survivors keep their will and all related papers for seven years. But check with the estate attorney to be double sure.

WHAT IS A LIVING TRUST?

You have probably heard a lot about the touted benefits of so-called "living trusts." Basically, these are trusts created during your lifetime where you retain control over the assets that are placed in the trust, but no longer own them.

Certainly, there are circumstances and individuals for whom a living trust is useful. But beware—far too often, people and organizations recommending living trusts may be more interested in generating fees than in objective estate planning for you.

Even if a living trust is established, you still need a will to deal with matters beyond the scope of the trust. You will never need a living trust without also having a will.

The living trust has some advantages, but it does not help you with federal estate tax. It helps you get privacy while you are alive and helps you avoid probate tax on the state level. A living trust does not make sense economically unless you have assets over $400,000, and it requires a lot of work.

I would suggest you consult an advisor specifically about your situation.

This definition is derived from Tennessee state law, but it probably is similar to the definition used in your state. For more legal information about estate planning, probate, wills and living trusts please visit CityLegalGuide.com.

The worst car accidents happen on the showroom floor!

I'm not against toys, just against toys eating your lunch. If you can't pay cash, you can't afford it.

AUTOMOBILES

AMERICANS have a "love-fest" going on with their cars. Where else can you find people flat broke, living paycheck to paycheck, with two vehicles in their driveway less than two years old? Ah, America. We love our cars!

The average monthly car payment is $378. If you only have one car payment you're shelling out almost $5,000 in one year. Investing $378 per month in a good growth stock mutual fund from age 25 to age 65 will be worth more than $4.4 million! A one-time $25,000 investment, leaving it sitting for thirty years (same terms) would net you more than $495,000! Hope you like your SUV!

Now make no mistake, I like cars. I have a couple of very nice ones, BUT, I paid cash for them and bought them when they were around two years old after some other lutz took the tail-kicking in depreciation. Cars drop over 40 percent in value in the first two years. Hmmmm. What else could you "invest" in that could fall that fast? Uh, maybe lead balloons!

Then there's "fleecing" a car, otherwise known to most people as leasing a car. Even *Consumer Reports* says that leasing a vehicle is one of the biggest rip-offs for the consumer. But, if you always want to have a payment, and you want to live like all the normal broke people, then by all means . . . lease a car. How silly!

So what do you do if you have a car payment? My rule-of-thumb is quite simple. If you can't pay it off in eighteen months . . . sell the car! Want to be broke all your life? Want to be normal? Normal is broke. If you want something better for your life, sell the car!

He who is waiting for something to "turn up"...
might start with his own shirt sleeves.
SAM WALTON

FOUR TIPS FOR BUYING A VEHICLE:

#1—Only buy a new car if you're very rich.

#2—Only drive a car that has taken its big hit in terms of depreciation—which means it's at least two years old—and then pay cash for it.

#3—If you currently have a car payment and you can't pay it off in eighteen months, then you need to sell the car and get rid of the debt. If the car sells for less than you owe, then you need to get a small loan from a credit union to cover the difference, plus another $2,000 so you can buy a junker for cash.

#4—Cars, trucks, boats, motorcycles, and other vehicles should not have a total value that exceeds half your annual income. If you make $60,000 and have two $30,000 cars, then no wonder you don't have any money.

MONEYMATTERS

SHOULD I BUY OR LEASE A CAR?

Leasing stinks. Here's why. Say that a brand new car sells for $18,000. If that car in four years loses 60 percent of its value, it would be worth $7,000. You've lost $11,000 in value. If you lease this car and bring it back to the dealer in four years and you have not paid them $11,000, then they have lost money. You have to pay them the depreciation in your payment or they lose money. They aren't in the business of losing money—so you've paid more than that $11,000 and have nothing to show for it.

If you could lease a car for less than it goes down in value, then it would make sense.

Food for thought: *Smart Money* magazine says the number one most profitable thing on the car lot is the financing contract. Number two is the repair shop. Number three is the extended warranty. Number four is the sale of vehicles. What kind of business are they in?! Buy a slightly used vehicle and you can get it for 25 percent off sticker. You'll always win this way.

Pro–lease people tend to rationalize about the benefits of "fleecing" because they want a new car. Only very rich people can afford to throw away money on new cars, and only people who don't do the math throw money away on fleecing.

WHY BUY A USED CAR INSTEAD OF A NEW ONE?

Buying a new car is not something 98 percent of the people out there need to be doing. It is a luxury item. Only buy a new car if you're filthy rich.

There are alternatives to buying new. Used lots are overflowing, and millions of cars come from expired leases.

The money saved by buying a used car is because of depreciation (the loss of the financial value of an object due to its use). Used cars have already depreciated (60 percent–70 percent in first four years). Buying used allows the person who bought the car when it was new to eat the cost of the depreciation. Then, the person who buys the car used can get a great car for much less than the new wholesale prices.

If you want to know what used cars are selling for these days, look online. I recommend the following sites:

· KBB.com

· Edmunds.com

· Carmax.com

Also, call some of the banks in your area and ask them how they dispose of their repossessions. If they have a repo auction in your area, this is a great way to find good deals.

But the best deals you can find are usually from individuals, because they are trying to get rid of their vehicles. Look in your area papers and find what's for sale.

BUT I REALLY, REALLY, REALLY WANT THAT CAR!

Before you take the plunge, listen.

When I went broke, my wife and I were sharing a car. My friend let me use a piece-of-junk car for a while. It was horrible! But, I was set in my mind to not borrow money. I ended up saving like crazy, and what I would have put into a car payment I ended up saving toward a new car. It was the best thing I could have done for myself.

You are looking into financing a sports car with payments of $400 per month. The car that you are driving now is worth around $1,500. If you take that $400 and pay yourself instead of paying it to the dealer, you will save $4,000 in 10 months. You will have $1,500 from selling your old car, so you will be able to buy a $5,500 car just 10 months from now. Continue doing that for another 10 months and you will be able to buy yourself a $10,000 car. That is only 20 months away. You can do it!

No car fever! Go take a cold shower! No new car!

CAN SOMEONE JUST TAKE OVER THE PAYMENTS ON A CAR LOAN?

When you put an ad in the paper asking for someone to take over your payments, it is like asking them to rent your car. This is not a good idea. Your name is still on the contract, and if the buyer quits paying, the creditors come for you.

Do not ever have someone take over your payments. Sell the car outright.

And don't just take over someone else's payments, either. If they weren't paying too much for the vehicle, they wouldn't be asking you to take over the payments. Find out what the car is worth, and buy it for that price.

You also might be able to refinance the car if you find someone to give you the loan, but this might not be worth it. First, I would call a credit union and refinance only if you can get a better interest rate.

HOW CAN I GET OUT OF MY CAR LEASE?

If you want to get out of a lease, you need to call the dealer and ask for what the early buyout amount is. Find out what this pay-off is and compare that to the value of the car.

Then, sell the car and compare that to the difference. You might need to come up with a couple extra thousand dollars. Borrow enough from your credit union to pay the lease off and an extra $1,000–$2,000 to buy a junker until you clean up the mess.

More people talk themselves into failure than talk themselves into success.
ZIG ZIGLAR

ARE EXTENDED WARRANTIES A GOOD DEAL?

Don't buy an extended warranty!

Extended warranties are insurance. Insurance has four parts: commission, overhead, statistical payout, and profit. Eighty-seven percent of the cost of the warranty covers commission, overhead, and profit. In other words, put 13 percent of what you would pay into the bank, and that will almost always cover the fixing of the item.

Self–insure your vehicle with an emergency fund, don't go to repair shops that rip you off, and don't buy extended warranties.

All vehicles have problems sometimes. That's just a fact of life. You need to talk to a mechanic, find out what the real problems are, and get a real cost estimate for the repairs. If your car is not too old, you should be able to keep it for a while. If you think you do not have the money to fix your car, then you certainly do not have the money to buy a different car. Put the money that you were placing toward your former car payment and place it toward the repairs.

MONEYMATTERS

Do you own your home?
Not until you pay off your mortgage
completely. This is the American
dream. Go for it!

Success is the intersection
where dreams and hard work meet.

LYNN GOLDBLATT

REAL ESTATE & MORTGAGES

REAL ESTATE is a favorite topic of a lot of people. It's not only fun to own real estate, but it's fun to invest in it. Do it well and it can be a major part of building wealth. Do it poorly and it can be a nightmare.

For individuals, I recommend that you only buy a house if you're out of debt, if you can put 20 percent down, and if your mortgage (including taxes and insurance) does not come to more than 25 percent of your household net (take home) income. I also recommend you pay cash for real estate, if at all possible.

Rental property is also a great way to generate income and build wealth, again, if done wisely.

If you have a mortgage the best thing you can do, after eliminating your consumer debt, fully funding an emergency fund, and getting your retirement and college funds going, is to pay off your house. Without a mortgage, you will have much more money to save and spend!

MONEYMATTERS

ARE WE READY TO BUY A HOUSE?

There are a few guidelines I suggest that you follow.

I do not suggest that you purchase a home until you have an emergency fund and are debt–free apart from your home.

Secondly, never do more than a 15–year mortgage.

Thirdly, I strongly recommend putting down at least 20 percent in order to avoid the PMI.

And fourth, your house payments should not be more than 1/4 of your take home pay. The interest rates being a little lower than usual is not a good reason to commit half of your income for a house payment. Wait until you're ready.

Also, I recommend that you don't buy a house in your first year of marriage—spend that time renting and building equity in your relationship before you undertake the additional responsibility of a house.

If you're thinking of buying a home with your boyfriend or girlfriend, don't do it! You should never buy homes with people you are not married to. You will create nightmares for yourself legally, morally, spiritually, and financially. It will be the worst mistake of your life.

HOW AGGRESSIVE SHOULD I BE ON PAYING OFF THE HOUSE?

Once you're free of other debts, it's very tempting to get real aggressive on your house payments. Some people are tempted to scale back on their 401(k) contributions in order to pay more on their mortgage.

But I would put 15 percent of my household income into retirement (baby step #4). After that, whatever extra I can afford, I'd throw into paying off the house.

If you've got extra money lying around, go ahead and put it into the mortgage, but don't scale back below 15 percent savings of total income for retirement. And don't cut into the emergency fund that covers three to six months of expenses.

Many mortgage companies will try to get you to sign up for a bi-weekly program in order to pay off your house faster, but you should never pay for a biweekly mortgage program. The reason why mortgage brokers say it pays off your house quicker is because you are paying twenty-six half payments per year, which results in thirteen full payments a year instead of twelve. I certainly advocate paying off your house early, but do it under your own discipline, not under a program designed by the mortgage broker.

CAN I QUALIFY FOR A MORTGAGE WITH NO CREDIT?

You have a credit history, even if you have no credit cards or car payments. You have rented a placed to live, and you've paid on time or early each month. Your mortgage broker needs to take five minutes to look at your credit history on paper rather than on the screen. Find someone who wants your business. You are doing great—no debt, no credit cards, no car payments, and one great credit history. Just find a mortgage broker who recognizes that—one who does manual underwriting and doesn't look only at credit scores—and you'll be set.

The first man gets the oyster, the second man gets the shell.
ANDREW CARNEGIE

WHICH IS BETTER—AN ADJUSTABLE OR FIXED RATE LOAN?

The adjustable rate is something you never do, while the fixed rate is something you should consider.

The fixed rate is easy to explain. The rate never changes as long as you have the mortgage. Simple!

The adjustable rate mortgages (ARMs) are horrible deals. The rates on these fluctuate drastically. They claim to give you a lower interest rate, but your risk is so high because of their fluctuation.

Stick with the fixed rate, and stick with a 15–year mortgage.

Those who aim low usually hit their targets.
Colin Powell

WHAT ARE 'POINTS' AND PMI?

One point equals one percent of the loan amount. Paying points or origination (another type of points) are not good plans. I recommend zero points and zero origination, otherwise what you are doing is prepaying interest and you usually don't get your money back quickly enough to justify doing it.

PMI (Private Mortage Insurance) is basically foreclosure insurance. This means that if you do not have at least 20 percent equity (meaning you did not put at least 20 percent down when you purchased the home), then they make you purchase insurance for the mortgage company which will cover any money they might lose through foreclosure. Monthly, this runs at about $70 per each $100,000 borrowed. You can get rid of this PMI if you pay the 20 percent up front, or if your home has gone up in value enough to cover it, which can only be proven through a standard appraisal.

WHAT IS AN 80/20 MORTGAGE AND IS IT A GOOD IDEA?

The best mortgage is the 100 percent down plan. No payments, no interest.

The 80/20 loan is when you take out an 80 percent mortgage to avoid PMI, but don't have 20 percent down. To cover the portion of the 20 percent down payment you don't have to get a small second mortgage. The theory of this is good (to dodge the PMI cost), but the second mortgage is usually a high interest rate, a variable interest rate, or has a balloon—any of which defeat the purpose of saving money by avoiding PMI.

You are better off to just take a 90 percent loan and pay PMI until you can get the loan to low enough to drop the PMI cost.

When you do things, don't let selfishness or pride be your guide. Instead, be humble and give more honor to others than to yourselves.
PHILIPPIANS 2:3 NCV

ABOUT DAVE, FPU, AND THE 'DAVE RAMSEY SHOW'

DAVE RAMSEY, a personal money management expert, is an extremely popular national radio personality and author of the *New York Times* best-sellers *The Total Money Makeover, Financial Peace,* and *More Than Enough*. Ramsey knows first-hand what financial peace means in his own life—living a true riches to rags to riches story. By age twenty-six he had established a four-million-dollar real estate portfolio, only to lose it by age thirty. He has since rebuilt his financial life and now devotes himself full-time to helping ordinary people understand the forces behind their financial distress and how to set things right—financially, emotionally, and spiritually. He resides with his wife, Sharon, and their three children in Nashville, Tennessee.

Among Dave's other books are:

The Total Money Makeover
The Total Money Makeover Workbook
The Total Money Training Plan
Priceless
More Than Enough
Financial Peace Revisited

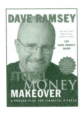 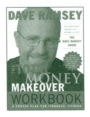

Millions of listeners hear Dave every weekday on *The Dave Ramsey Show*—"Where life happens, caller after caller." LIVE 2–5 EST

MyTotalMoneyMakeover.com—Ever wished you could tap into Dave's financial advice 24/7? Now you can!

Financial Peace University is the most important step to changing your financial future. It is your Total Money Makeover Program! It takes the head knowledge from the books and the radio show and turns it into real action. FPU is a 13-week life-changing program that empowers and teaches you how to make the right money decisions to achieve your financial goals and experience a total money makeover. More than 100,000 families and individuals have attended FPU at their workplace, church, military base, non-profit organization, or community group.

For more information about these and Dave's other resources, please visit *www.daveramsey.com*

The bridge between failure and success is HOPE.

THOMAS JEFFERSON

We also glory in tribulations, knowing that tribulation produces perseverance; and perseverance, character; and character, hope. Now hope does not disappoint, because the love of God has been poured out in our hearts by the Holy Spirit who was given to us.

ROMANS 5:3–5 NKJV

YOU CAN DO IT!